T0209115

国家汉办/孔子学院总部
Hanban/Confucius Institute Headquarters

Mozi

Collection of Critical Biographies of Chinese Thinkers

(Concise Edition, Chinese-English)

Editors-in-chief: Zhou Xian, Cheng Aimin

Author: Zheng Jiewen, Zhang Qian
Translator: David B.Honey
Expert: Li Ji

Nanjing University Press

《中国思想家评传》简明读本 - 中英文版 -
主 编 周 宪 程爱民

墨 子

著 者 / 郑杰文 Zheng Jiewen
　　　 张 倩 Zhang Qian
译 者 / David B. Honey
审 读 / 李 寄 Li Ji

南京大学出版社

Editor: Rui Yimin
Cover designed by Zhao Qin

First published 2010
by Nanjing University Press
No. 22, Hankou Road, Nanjing City, 210093
www.NjupCo.com

©2010 Nanjing University Press

Chinese Library Cataloguing in Publication Data
The CIP data for this title is on file with the Chinese Library.

ISBN10: 7-305-07970-2(pbk)
ISBN13: 978-7-305-07970-2(pbk)

Books available in the collection

Confucius
《孔子》
978-7-305-06611-5

Laozi
《老子》
978-7-305-06607-8

Emperor Qin Shihuang
《秦始皇》
978-7-305-06608-5

Li Bai
《李白》
978-7-305-06609-2

Cao Xueqin
《曹雪芹》
978-7-305-06610-8

Du Fu
《杜甫》
978-7-305-06826-3

Zhuangzi
《庄子》
978-7-305-07177-5

Sima Qian
《司马迁》
978-7-305-07294-9

Mencius
《孟子》
978-7-305-07583-4

Mozi
《墨子》
978-7-305-07970-2

总序

General Preface

China is one of the cradles of world civilization, enjoying over five thousand years of history. It has produced many outstanding figures in the history of ancient thought, and left a rich philosophical heritage for both the Chinese people and the entire humanity. The fruit of these thinkers was to establish unique schools that over the long course of history have been continuously interpreted and developed. Today much of these thoughts are as relevant as ever and of extreme vitality for both China and the rest of the world. For instance, the ideal of "humaneness" and the concept of "harmony" taught by Confucius, the founder of Confucianism, have been venerated without ceasing by contemporary China as well as other Asian nations.

Ancient Chinese dynasties came and went, with each new dynasty producing its own scintillating system of thought. These rare and beautiful flowers of philosophy are grounded in the hundred schools vying for attention in pre-Qin times and the broad yet deep classical scholarship of Han and Tang times and in the simple yet profound occult learning of the Wei and Jin dynasties together with the entirely rational learning of Song and Ming Neo-Confucianism. The fertile soil of religious belief was Buddhism's escape from the emptiness of the sensual world and Daoism's spiritual cultivation in the search for identification with the immortals. The founders of these systems of thought included teachers, scholars, poets, politicians, scientists and monks— they made great contributions to such disparate cultural fields in ancient China as philosophy, politics, military science, economics, law, handicrafts, science and technology, literature, art, and religion. The ancient Chinese venerated them for their wisdom and for following moral paths, and called them sages, worthies, saints, wise men, and great masters, etc. Their words and writings, and sometimes their life experiences, constitute the rich matter of ancient Chinese thought distilled by later generations. The accomplishments of Chinese thought are rich and varied, and permeate such spiritual traditions as the harmony between humans and nature, the unification of thought and action, and the need for calmness during vigorous action, synthesizing the old and innovating something new.

Nanjing University Press has persisted over the last twenty years in publishing the 200-book series, *Collection of Critical Biographies of Chinese Thinkers*, under the general editorship of Professor Kuang Yaming, late honorary president of Nanjing University. This collection is the largest-scale project of research on Chinese thinking and culture undertaken since the beginning of the twentieth century. It selected more than 270 outstanding figures from Chinese history, composed their biographies and criticized their

中国是世界文明的发源地之一,有五千多年的文明史。在中国古代思想史上,涌现出了许许多多杰出的思想家,为中华民族乃至整个人类留下了丰富的思想遗产。这些思想成果独树一帜,在漫长的历史中又不断地被阐释、被发展,很多思想对于今天的中国乃至世界而言,仍然历久弥新,极具生命力。比如,儒家学派创始人孔子"仁"的理念、"和"的思想,不仅在当代中国,在其他亚洲国家也一直备受推崇。

古代中国朝代更迭,每一个朝代都有灿烂夺目的思想文化。百家争鸣的先秦诸子、博大宏深的汉唐经学、简易幽远的魏晋玄学、尽心知性的宋明理学是思想学术的奇葩;佛教的色空禅悦、道教的神仙修养是宗教信仰的沃土;其他如经世济民的政治、经济理想,巧夺天工的科技、工艺之道,风雅传神、丹青不老的文学艺术……都蕴涵着丰富的思想。这些思想的创造者中有教师、学者、诗人、政治家、科学家、僧人……他们在中国古代的哲学、政治、军事、经济、法律、工艺、科技、文学、艺术、宗教等各个文明领域内贡献巨大。古代中国人尊敬那些充满智慧、追求道德的人,称呼他们为圣人、贤人、哲人、智者、大师等,他们的言论、著作或被后人总结出来的经验构成了中国古代思想的重要内容,在丰富多彩中贯穿着天人合一、知行合一、刚健中和等精神传统,表现出综合创新的特色。

南京大学出版社坚持20余年,出版了由南京大学已故名誉校长匡亚明教授主编的《中国思想家评传丛书》,这套丛书共200部,是中国20世纪以来最为宏大的中国传统思想文化研究工程,选出了中国历史上270余位杰出人物,为他们写传记,

intellectual accomplishments; all in all, it is a rigorous and refined academic work. On this foundation, we introduce this series of concise readers, which provides much material in a simple format. It includes the cream of the crop of great figures relatively familiar to foreign readers. We have done our best to use plain but vivid language to narrate their human stories of interest; this will convey the wisdom of their thought and display the cultural magnificence of the Chinese people. In the course of spiritually communing with these representative thinkers from ancient China, readers will certainly be able to apprehend the undying essence of thoughts of the Chinese people.

Finally, we are deeply grateful for the support from Hanban/ Confucius Institute Headquarters, and the experts from home and abroad for their joint efforts in writing and translating this series.

Editors
November, 2009

评论他们的思想成就，是严肃精深的学术著作。在此基础上推出的这套简明读本，则厚积薄发，精选出国外读者相对较为熟悉的伟大人物，力求用简洁生动的语言，通过讲述有趣的人物故事，传达他们的思想智慧，展示中华民族绚烂多姿的文化。读者在和这些中国古代有代表性的思想家的心灵对话中，一定能领略中华民族思想文化生生不息的精髓。

最后，我们衷心感谢国家汉办/孔子学院总部对本项目提供了巨大的支持，感谢所有参与此套丛书撰写和翻译工作的中外专家学者为此套丛书所做的辛勤而卓有成效的工作。

编者
2009年11月

目录

Contents

Chapter I   Independent Warlords All Arise, a Rare Talent in an
               Age of Chaos: The Cultural Origin and Social
               Background of the Creation of Mohism -------------- 1
Chapter II   Abandoning Confucianism and Establishing
               Mohism, Tirelessly Doing Good: Mozi's Life Story
               and Campaign Against Warfare -------------------- 9
Chapter III   The Torch of Learning is Passed Down, the New
               Generation Improves on the Old: Later Mohist
               Schools and Activities ---------------------------- 29
Chapter IV   All-Embracing Learning, a Unique School of
               Thought: The Major Works of Mohism -------------- 49
Chapter V   Pursuing True Knowledge, Unusual Luster Exhibited
               in Profusion: The Major Accomplishments of the
               "Mohist Canon" ---------------------------------- 63
Chapter VI   Frugality Leads to Flourishing, Indulgence Leads to
               Destruction: Mohist Economic Thought ------------- 79
Chapter VII   Embracing Universal Love, Engaging in What is
               Mutually Beneficial: The Ethical Thinking of
               Mohism -- 89
Chapter VIII   Against Offensive Warfare and Saving through
               Defensive Warfare, Aggressive Defense: Mohist
               Military Thought ----------------------------------101
Chapter IX   Venerate Heaven and Serve Ghosts, Setting up
               Religion to Teach the Way of the Spirits: Religious
               Doctrines of Mohism ------------------------------113
Chapter X   Powerful Teaching and Powerful Learning,
               Practicing What He Preached: Mozi's Educational
               Thought --125
Chapter XI   Founder of Materialism, Profound Thinker and
               Skilled Debater: The "Three Criteria" of Mohism ------145
Chapter VII   Meritocracy and the Advocacy of Unity: Mozi's
               Political Thought --------------------------------151
Chapter XIII   From Apogee to Decline, after Misfortune Comes
               Good Fortune: The Decline and Renaissance of
               Mohism ---163
Chapter XIV   A Thousand Years of Continuity, His Undying Spirit:
               The Influence of Mohism -------------------------183
Translator's Note ---190

一 群雄并起，乱世奇葩
  ——墨学产生的文化渊源与社会背景 ………………………… 1

二 弃儒立墨，行义不倦
  ——墨子的生平事迹与止战游说 …………………………… 9

三 薪尽火传，后来居上
  ——墨家后学的派别及活动 ………………………………… 29

四 包罗万象，独树一帜
  ——墨家的主要著作 ………………………………………… 49

五 探求真知，异彩纷呈
  ——《墨经》的主要成就 …………………………………… 63

六 俭节则昌，淫佚则亡
  ——墨家的经济思想 ………………………………………… 79

七 兼相爱，交相利
  ——墨家的伦理思想 ………………………………………… 89

八 非攻救守，积极防御
  ——墨家的军事思想 ………………………………………… 101

九 尊天事鬼，神道设教
  ——墨家的宗教学说 ………………………………………… 113

十 强教强学，言传身教
  ——墨家的教育思想 ………………………………………… 125

十一 唯物师祖，精思巧辩
  ——墨家的"三表法" ……………………………………… 145

十二 任人唯贤，倡导统一
  ——墨家的政治思想 ………………………………………… 151

十三 由盛而衰，否极泰来
  ——墨学的衰亡与复兴 ……………………………………… 163

十四 绵延千年，精神不灭
  ——墨学的影响 ……………………………………………… 183

译后记 ……………………………………………………………… 190

一　群雄并起，乱世奇葩
——墨学产生的文化渊源与社会背景

Chapter I　Independent Warlords All Arise, a Rare Talent in an Age of Chaos: The Cultural Origin and Social Background of the Creation of Mohism

During the Spring and Autumn and Warring States Periods, because of the ceaseless development of the art of forging iron and the broad utilization of iron tools, agriculture, handicrafts and trade rapidly developed. According to what written records and underground discoveries made through archeology tell us, in the Spring and Autumn and Warring States Periods, iron implements had already gradually replaced the crude tools of production from earlier ages, and were broadly utilized in agricultural production; this accelerated development in agricultural production. The universal utilization of iron agricultural implements made it possible for the plowing of fields to be undertaken across large areas, and also created the necessary conditions for building irrigation works on a large scale. The spread of the use of iron agricultural implements and the building of irrigation works also provided rather fine production conditions for self-employment in agriculture, promoting ceaseless improvement in the techniques of agricultural production. The gradual spread of cultivation by ox plow caused farming techniques to make striking advances, and meticulous techniques for "deep plowing and easy weeding" step by step became realized. And the widespread popularization of iron implements for use in handicraft labor provided sharp and effective tools, so handicraft production in each state and region manifested striking progress.

The rapid development and ceaseless social division of labor in agriculture and handicrafts directly brought about unprecedented stimulation in trade and the exchange of currency, and also caused the enlargement of the scale of cities on an almost daily basis. The capital cities of each state such as Linzi, Handan, Luoyang and the like gradually formed commercial centers. The monopoly enjoyed since the Western Zhou of "officials being used to feed labor and trade" had been destroyed, and a class of merchants engaging in trade activities gradually developed and expanded, producing such famous merchants as Xian Gao and Fan Li.

Following the development of production forces and improvements in the tools of production, uncultivated land, as apart from government owned land, became exploited on a large scale, so the scope of privately owned fields increased without ceasing. This led to the unending development of the system of private ownership of land, and the well system started to fragment and get worse day by day; what replaced it was the aid system which was more suited to the development of the forces of production. The small production unit of one family and one household was far superior to the collective labor of the slave system, which promoted development along the lines of small agricultural production units.

春秋战国时期，由于冶铁技术的不断进步和铁制工具的广泛使用，农业、手工业和商业得到迅速发展。据文献记载和地下考古发掘表明，在春秋战国时期，铁器已逐步代替以前的粗笨生产工具，广泛应用于农业生产，从而促进了农业生产的大发展。铁制农具的普遍使用，使大面积的农田耕作成为可能，也为大规模的兴修水利创造了必要条件。铁制农具的推广和水利的兴修，又给农业的个体劳动提供了较好的生产条件，促进了农业生产技术的不断进步。牛耕的渐次推广，使耕作技术得到显著提高，农业生产中的"深耕易耨"的精细化生产也逐步得以实现。而铁器的广泛应用也为手工业劳动提供了锐利而有效的工具，各个国家和地区的手工业生产都呈现出突飞猛进的形势。

农业、手工业的飞速发展和社会分工的不断扩大直接带来了商业、货币往来的空前活跃，也使得城市规模日益扩大。各国都城，如临淄、邯郸、洛阳等，逐渐形成为商业中心。西周以来"工商食官"的垄断局面已被打破，独立从事商业活动的商人阶层逐步发展壮大，出现了不少如弦高、范蠡一样的著名商人。

随着生产力的发展和生产工具的改进，公田之外的大量荒地得到开垦，私田范围不断扩大。由此导致土地私有制不断发展，井田制日益瓦解，取而代之的是更适应生产力发展的爰田制，这种一家一户为单位的小生产远胜于奴隶制的集体劳动，从而促进了农业小生产方式的发展。

Under this type of historical condition, production relationships of feudalism that were suitable for the development of new production forces started to appear and gradually expanded. Contradictions and struggles between new production relationships fundamentally shook the ruling order of the slave system, inciting struggles for political rights among slave-owning aristocracy, and between slave-owning aristocracy and the newly formed landlord class. Feudal lords vied for supremacy and independent warlords rose up, and the wheel of history in that chaotic age ineluctably rolled along. The political system, economic structure and cultural orientation of society also changed in broad and profound ways in the fierce turbulence of the times. Blocs ceaseless expanded that had been formed out of various groups such as were formed when slaves were liberated and became free people, and when small handicraft industries and petty merchants formed from the disparity between rich and poor; such blocs gradually formed a relatively independent class. They started to express their own political leanings, and sought their own independent political positions. Mozi was a representative of this particular class.

According to the research of a scholar from Shandong, Mr. Zhang Zhihan, Mozi was born in Lanyi in the state of Zhu. Linyi was a vassal state of Song, Song being the homeland where descendants of Shang royalty had been settled. Later on, Zhu became a dependency of Lu, so many historical sources regard Mozi as being from Lu. Because Zhu lined both banks of the Si River in Shandong, its land was fertile and climate mild, thus enjoying superior natural endowments. Therefore, this entire stretch has always been a region of comparatively developed material and spiritual cultures, and produced the splendid Zhulou culture. The so-called Zhulou culture actually was part of the culture of the Yan ethnic group (that is, the culture of the eastern indigenous people the Dongyi). Since the time of Tang and Yu up until the early Zhou, the Zhulou culture had always led the way for the cultures of other ethnic groups, becoming an important source for Chinese culture. Since antiquity, the Zhulou region has been called "the homeland of all craftsmen." Many implements associated in antiquity with clothing, food, dwelling and transportation were invented or created by men of Zhulou, and Zhulou scientific technology clearly led the way at the time. Only a region with such a grounding in science and technology could have produced such a great master of science and technology as Mozi. In addition to this, Zhulou historically had the customs of "venerating Heaven, revering ancestors, honoring ghosts and spirits, esteeming doctors

在这种历史条件下，适应新生产力发展的封建制的生产关系开始出现并逐步扩大。新旧生产关系的矛盾和斗争从根本上动摇了奴隶制的统治秩序，引起了奴隶主贵族内部、奴隶主贵族和新兴地主阶级之间政治权利的争夺。诸侯争霸、群雄并起，历史的车轮在摧枯拉朽般的动乱中滚滚向前。社会的政治制度、经济结构和文化取向也在激烈的动荡中发生着广泛而深刻的变革。由于奴隶解放而形成的自由民和由于贫富分化而形成的小手工业者、小商人等组成的集团不断壮大，逐步形成了一个相对独立的阶层，他们开始拥有自己的政治主张，并且寻求独立的政治地位。墨子就是这一阶层的代表。

据山东学者张知寒先生考证，墨子出生在小邾国的滥邑。滥邑，原为商的遗裔宋国的附庸，后来成为鲁的属地，所以史料多以墨子为鲁人。由于地处泗水两岸，土地肥沃、气候温和，自然条件十分优越，因此这一带一直是物质文化和精神文化比较发达的地区，并产生出灿烂辉煌的邾娄文化。所谓邾娄文化，其实就是炎族文化（即东夷文化）的一部分。自唐、虞以至周初，邾娄文化就一直领先于其他各族文化，成为华夏文化的主要源头之一。邾娄地区自古就有"百工之乡"的称号，古代衣食住行的许多器物也都由邾娄人发明创造，科学技术在当时一直遥遥领先。唯有这样的科技之邦，才能铸就出墨子这样伟大的科技人物。此外，邾娄地区历来就有"尊天、敬祖，重鬼神，

who used both spells and herbs, and not competing for material gain." ❶ From this, Zhulou formulated a culture of ethics based on benefitting others, humaneness, and love. All of this formulated the source of Mozi's thought.

When Mozi was born, the small state of Zhu had already become a dependency of Lu. At the time, the lord and ministers of Lu were enjoying lives of extravagance and dissipation, indulging in pleasure and wallowing in debauchery all day long. Among the common people, "those who were hungry had nothing to eat, those who were cold had nothing to wear, those who labored could not rest." ❷ This means that during times of famine there was no food to be found to fill stomachs; during times of cold there was no clothing to warm the body; during times of hard work it was impossible to be able to rest. Throughout the whole society, "the strong pillaged the weak, the many tyrannized the few, the devious cheated the innocent, the noble lorded over the lowly." ❸ When the strong pillaged the weak, the many with power in numbers tyrannized the few with no power, the devious and tricky cheated the innocent and the simple, and the noble and prominent lorded over the lowly and base; this demonstrates that society had already reached the level when "the rites had collapsed and music had decayed." Royal princes and grandsons struggled year after year, and such states as Qi and Yue stared covetously at Lu with the fierce eyes of a tiger, and attacked cities and plundered the land on numerous occasions. The state had fallen into a condition of facing rebellion from within and attack from without.

In the midst of such tumult, royal power step by step declined, and government-run schools gradually found it difficult to keep operating. A natural result of this was the rise and flourishing of private schools. Given this background of "the Son of Heaven having lost power and learning having shifted to the barbarous tribes all around," small producers gained the opportunity to study cultural knowledge; that is, they gained the opportunity to rise to the ranks of the scholars. Mozi was just such a sage from among the common people who arose in response to the needs of times from the lowly background of a small producer. What he advocated for saving the state included in the main "Universal Love," "Against Offensive Warfare," "Elevating the Worthy," "Identifying with One's Superior," "Will of Heaven," "Explaining Ghosts," "Frugality in Expenditures," "Frugal Burials," "Against Music," and "Against Fate." He and his disciples made great achievements in science and logic. His ideal of being willing to "undergo any hardship for the sake of the good" ❹ displayed a lofty character. All of this made him and the Mohist school which he founded become a dazzling and rare flower in an age of transformation.

尚祝由，与物无竞"❶的风俗，进而形成了以利他、仁爱为特色的伦理文化，这些都成为了墨子思想的渊源。

墨子出生时，小邾国已成为鲁国的属地。当时的鲁国，君臣骄奢淫逸，宴乐终日，花天酒地。平民百姓"饥者不得食，寒者不得衣，劳者不得息"❷，也就是说在饥饿时得不到可以果腹的粮食，天寒时没有可以御寒的冬衣，筋疲力尽时也没有可能休息。整个社会"强之劫弱，众之暴寡，诈之谋愚，贵之敖贱"❸。已经到了强者劫掠弱者，人多势众的欺负势单力薄的，奸诈的人欺骗憨厚的人，显贵的人傲视低贱的人这样一种"礼崩乐坏"的地步。而王室子孙连年争斗，齐、越等国都对鲁国虎视眈眈，多次攻城掠地。国家陷入了内忧外患之中。

王权在动荡中一步步走向衰落，官办的学校逐渐难以为继，随之而起的是私人办学的兴盛。在这种"天子失官，学在四夷"的背景下，小生产者有了学习文化知识的可能，也就有了上升为士的机会。墨子就是在这种背景下应运而生的一位出身低贱、为小生产者立言的平民圣人。他的以"兼爱"、"非攻"、"尚贤"、"尚同"、"天志"、"明鬼"，"节用"、"节葬"、"非乐"、"非命"为主要内容的救国主张，他和弟子在科学、逻辑学中所取得的伟大成就，他的"摩顶放踵利天下，为之"❹。的高尚人格，使他和他所创立的墨学成为那一变革时代中一朵耀眼的奇葩。

❶ 参见张知寒等：《墨子里籍考论》，山东人民出版社，1996年，第7页。
❷ 《墨子·非乐上》，以下引《墨子》只注篇名。
❸ 《兼爱下》。
❹ 《孟子·尽心上》。

❶ Consult Zhang Zhihan et al., *A Technical Discussion of Mozi's Native Place*, Shandong People's Publishing House, 1996, p. 7.
❷ *Mozi*, "Against Music," Part One. Below I will not mention the book *Mozi*, but only cite the names of particular chapters.
❸ "Universal Love," Part Three.
❹ *Mencius*, "Jinxin," Part One.

墨子画像
Portrait of Mozi

二 弃儒立墨，行义不倦

——墨子的生平事迹与止战游说

Chapter II Abandoning Confucianism and Establishing Mohism, Tirelessly Doing Good: Mozi's Life Story and Campaign Against Warfare

Mozi's name was Di; legend has it that his mother dreamed of a phoenix entering her chamber; when she woke she gave birth to him and named him Di (a large bird). But later on many other versions surfaced. During the Yuan Dynasty in his *Library of the Celestial Ruler*, Yi Shizhen cited the *Collection of Sayings by Master Jia* to the effect that Mozi was not surnamed Mo, but was surnamed Di, with the name of Wu. Zhou Lianggong of the Qing Dynasty also supported this theory in his *Book Reproductions from the Hut Among the Trees*. But the Republican era scholar Qian Mu felt instead that the reason Mozi was called Master Mo, "the Inky Master," was that he had been punished by being tattooed with ink. In addition to this, someone said that the reason he was called "Inky" was that his skin had been sunburned due to having been constantly on the go. Another theory as to why he was called "Inky" was about his skill in using the chalk line stained with ink employed by carpenters and was himself a highly skilled carpenter.

The reason there are so many competing theories about even the most basic information about Mozi, like his surname, is the lack of historical materials. In the work authored by Sima Qian, *Records of the Grand Historian*, he included rather lengthy biographies of Confucius, Mencius, Laozi and Zhuangzi. Only his treatment of Mozi is vague at best, and only in the tail end of the "Biographies of Mencius and Xunzi" did he write with a conjectural tone that "It seems that Mo Di was a grandee of the state of Song who was skilled in defensive warfare and practiced frugality. Some say he was a contemporary of Confucius, some say he was later." This short passage of only 24 characters cannot possibly describe the complete life of such a great figure as Mozi.

As for his birthplace, there are even more competing theories, with scholars across the ages each holding to different views. The following three theories are the major ones:

First, the Song theory. In the *Records of the Grand Historian*, it records that "Mo Di was a grandee from Song," stating clearly that he was an official from the state of Song; many argue on this basis that Mozi came from the state of Song, that is, he was a native of the modern region of Shangqiu in Henan. This is just what Ge Hong of the Eastern Jin Dynasty stated in his *Biographies of Immortals*: "Mozi was named Di, a man of Song." Li Bao of the Tang Dynasty, in his work *Census of Surnames During the Yuanhe Era*, not only mentioned that Mozi was a native of Song, but also confirmed the derivation of the Mo clan: "The Mo clan was made up of descendants of Lord Guzhu, and was originally called the Motai clan; later it changed into the Mo clan whose

墨子，名翟，传说中墨子的母亲分娩前曾梦到有凤凰入室，醒来生下墨子，故而给他取名翟（音dí，大鸟）。但后世却多有异说。元代伊世珍在《琅嬛记》中引用《贾子说林》，称墨子并非姓墨，而是姓翟名乌；清代周亮工在《因树屋书影》一书中亦持此论。而民国学者钱穆则认为，墨子之所以叫墨子，是因为他曾受过墨刑。此外，有人说墨子是因为终日奔波而使皮肤变得黝黑，才被称作"墨"。也有人认为"墨"是木匠艺人用来打线的绳墨，而墨子是一位技艺精湛的木匠，因为他有着出色的绳墨技巧而被人称之为"墨"。

之所以连最基本的姓氏都有如此纷繁的说法，都是因为史料的阙佚。司马迁著《史记》，对孔子、孟子、老子、庄子均有较长传记，唯独对墨子语焉不详，仅在《孟子荀卿列传》末尾以推测的语气写道："盖墨翟，宋之大夫，善守御，为节用。或曰并孔子时，或曰在其后。"这区区二十四个字，根本无法描绘出墨子这样一个伟大人物的生平全貌。

关于墨子的籍贯，更是众说纷纭，历来学者所见也各不相同。大致有以下三种说法：

一、宋人说。《史记》中载"墨翟，宋大夫也"，说墨子是宋国的大夫，有人据此认为墨子就是宋国人，即今河南商丘人。如东晋葛洪在《神仙传》中说："墨子者名翟，宋人也。"唐人林宝的《元和姓纂》不仅说墨子是宋人，而且还考证了墨氏的

members were natives of Song during the Warring States Period. Mo Di composed a book called *Mozi*."

Second, the Chu theory. A passage from the *Huainanzi*, "Fanlun" states, "Summarizing the Confucians and Mohists from Zou and Lu, they were able to master the transmitted teachings of the previous sages." In his *Preface to Annotations on Mozi*, Bi Yuan explained that the mention of "Lu" in this passage referred to Luyang of the state of Chu, that is, modern Lushan county in He'nan province. The *Postlude to Mozi* of Wu Yi also supports this viewpoint.

Third, the Lu theory. In the annotations to two chapters of the *Spring and Autumn Annals of Mr. Lü*, the "What Should be Dyed" and the "Shenda" sections, the Eastern Han scholar Gao You regarded Mozi as a man of Lu. The Qing scholar Sun Yirang even more clearly confirmed that Mozi "was born in Lu and served in Song" in his work *Annotations on Mozi*, "Postface on Mozi, Part One."

At present, most scholars regard Mozi as being a man from the state of Lu of the Warring States Period. His ancestor was the eldest son of the older brother of Duke Xiang of Song, and was therefore set up in his own feudal state in Muyi; he hence was called Master Muyi. Muyi originally was a small regional state set up during the Shang Dynasty for a member of the royal clan. After Zhou succeeded the Shang it was amalgamated with the small state of Zhulou, which is now within the boundaries of Tengzhou city, Shandong province.

As for the birth and death dates of Mozi, no unanimous conclusions have been reached by academics. In his *Records of the Grand Historian*, Sima Qian wrote ambiguously "some say he was a contemporary of Confucius, some say that he came later," leaving a riddle for the ages. Scholars are only able to roughly deduce a period of his being born sometime before 476 B.C., and dying sometime before 390 B.C., in the general period after the death of Confucius and before the birth of Mencius.

Mozi's background was that of a commoner; he called himself "a rustic from the north" [1] and others called him "a knight of the commoners" [2] and a "base man." [3] Because his family was poor, he was forced to learn some manual skills when he was young to make a living. His natural intelligence in addition to what he learned through his own diligence, quickly made him a

由来："墨氏，孤竹君之后，本墨台氏，后改为墨氏，战国时宋人。墨翟著书号《墨子》。"

二、楚人说。《淮南子·氾论》有言："总邹鲁之儒墨，通先圣之遗教。"清代毕沅在《墨子注序》中将"鲁"解释为楚国的鲁阳，也就是今天的河南省鲁山县。武亿的《跋墨子》也持同样观点。

三、鲁人说。东汉末年的高诱在《吕氏春秋》的《当染》和《慎大》两篇的注文中都认为墨子是鲁国人。清代学者孙诒让在《墨子间诂·墨子后语上》中更明确指出墨子"生于鲁而仕于宋"。

目前，一般认为墨子是春秋战国时期鲁国人。他的祖先是宋襄公之兄的长子，因封于目夷，所以名"目夷子"。目夷原为商朝所建的同姓小方国，入周之后被并入小邾娄国，在今山东省滕州市境内。

关于墨子的生卒年也是学术界莫衷一是的问题，司马迁在《史记》中含糊其辞地写下"或曰并孔子时，或曰在其后"，给后人留下了千古一谜。学者们只能大致推定墨子生于公元前476年左右，卒于公元前390年左右，大致在孔子逝世之后、孟子出生之前的这一段时间。

墨子出身平民，自称"北方之鄙人"[1]，人称"布衣之士"[2]和"贱人"[3]。由于家境贫寒，在少年时代他不得不学习一些手工技艺以维生。他聪慧的天资再加上后天的勤奋，使

---

[1]《吕氏春秋·爱类》。
[2]《吕氏春秋·博志》。
[3]《吕氏春秋·贵义》。

[1] *Spring and Autumn Annals of Mr. Lü*, "Ailei."
[2] *Spring and Autumn Annals of Mr. Lü*, "Bozhi."
[3] *Spring and Autumn Annals of Mr. Lü*, "Guiyi."

master of manual skills. According to the *Han Feizi*, "Waichu," Mozi once crafted a wooden kite that was able to stay aloft for an entire day; all of his students could not help but praise it, saying, "Master, your skills are marvelous! You can even make a wooden kite fly!" But Mozi felt that it was not as good as making a cart with the materials right at hand within one day that could hold 30 *dan* of goods, and that could be used for a long time. In addition to this, Mozi also had mastered the principles and methods of manufacturing machinery, and was able to design and manufacture many different kinds of defensive weapons used in siege warfare. Therefore, during the Warring States Period even the rhetorician and debator Hui Shi praised "Mozi's great skills." In more colloquial terms, Mozi can be described as a master craftsman.

Even after he had mastered his craft, he was not satisfied with the artisanship of his "great skills;" he also had great desires to master knowledge in other realms. According to the account of the *Spring and Autumn Annals of Mr. Lü*, "What Should be Dyed," in order to express his respect for the Zhou Son of Heaven, Duke Hui of Lu sent the grandee Zai Rang to King Huan of Zhou to ask about the rituals associated with the suburban temple sacrifice. So King Huan sent an official named Jue to the state of Lu. Later, Jue was detained in Lu by Duke Hui; his descendants thereafter flourished in Lu. Mozi studied these rites with these descendants. So the Confucians who exerted a great influence on Lu at the time were the ones who enlightened Mozi during his early educational years.

When Mozi was born, the minor state of Zhu where his homeland was located was a subordinate state of Lu. Lu preserved the most rituals from the Zhou court, and furthermore was the area in which Confucian thought had spread the widest. The *Huainanzi*, "Yaolue," reported: "Mozi followed the profession of the scholars, and received the traditions of Confucius." This is clearly evident in the *Mozi*, which repeatedly cites the contents of the *Book of Poetry* and the *Book of History*; and historical figures and allusions from the *Spring and Autumn Annals* appear throughout the book. In addition, it also analyzed and criticized the content of rites and music, and absorbed them in the book. From this it is evident that in his heart Mozi probably admired Confucian theories very highly.

Nevertheless, the age in which he lived and his derivation from a "base" background sealed his fate, preventing him from following the traditional path of a Confucian. Because of his background as a commoner, since a young age Mozi was able to experience the normal social vicissitudes associated with the lowest levels of society; his experience studying a craft further let him

他很快成为手工技艺一流的人物。据《韩非子·外储说》记载，墨子曾制造过一只木鸢，能在空中飞翔一日，他的学生都禁不住称赞："先生的手艺多么神巧啊！竟能使木鸢飞起来！"墨子却认为这还不如他制造的车子，用咫尺之木，不到一天便可完工，却能承载三十石的货物，而且还能长期使用。除此之外，墨子还精通机械制造的原理和方法，能够设计并制作多种守城的防御器械。因而，连战国时代著名的名辩家惠施都赞叹"墨子大巧"。用通俗的话说，就是墨子真是一个能工巧匠。

学有所成之后，墨子并没有满足于自己的"大巧"之艺，他对其他知识也有着强烈的渴求。《吕氏春秋·当染》记载，当年鲁惠公为了表示对周天子的尊重，曾经派大夫宰让到周桓王那里请教有关郊庙的礼仪，周桓王就派了一名叫"角"的史官前往鲁国。后来角被惠公留在了鲁国，他的后代便在鲁国繁衍生息，墨子就向角的后代学习这些礼仪。而在当时对鲁国影响极大的儒学，更是墨子早期教育的启蒙者。

在墨子出生时，他的家乡所在的小邾国已成为鲁的属国。鲁国保存周礼最多，又是儒家学说广为流传的地区。因此，墨子自幼便受儒家文化的熏陶，他曾经投身孔门，学习过儒术。《淮南子·要略》就说："墨子学儒者之业，受孔子之术。"这从《墨子》书中可以明显看出，它对《诗》、《书》中的内容有反复引述，《春秋》中的人物、典故也随处可见。此外，它对《礼》、《乐》的内容也进行了深入分析和批判并加以吸收。由此可见，墨子内心对儒家学说应该是十分向往的。

然而，墨子所处的时代和他的"贱民"身份注定了他不可能再走儒者的老路。由于出身平民，墨子从小就能接触社会底层的沧桑百态，年少时的学艺经历又让他切身体会到了劳动人

personally go through the pains and sufferings of the laboring class of people. Therefore, early on he developed the ideals of changing what was unreasonable about reality and relieving the people from the sufferings of life. He devoted himself to his studies, hoping to find within Confucian theory a way to save the world. But after the death of Confucius, disciples of the various sects all fell into the trap of such trivial matters of ritual as "which direction to face, how to respond correctly, and how to enter and exit with deportment;" few were concerned with the life of the people. These rituals that were not connected to the life of the people provoked a greater and greater aversion in Mozi. He started to realize that it was not practical to try to save the world through worrying about the details of ritual, and that "obsessing over the rites brought worry, lavish funerals and extravagant wasting of resources impoverished the people, long mourning harmed life and impeded affairs." ❶ Such were his laments. Therefore, he resolutely abandoned Confucianism and established his own school of thought— Mohism.

After establishing this school, Mozi took "promoting the benefits to all the world, and eliminating all the harm in the world" ❷ as his own duty. The scale of his school rapidly grew, and the influence of Mohist theory deepened each day. In that period when he was calling on others to serve and recruiting disciples, each ruler of the various states wanted to utilize the power of Mozi to serve their states. In order to save the people from dire straits, on one hand Mozi recruited disciples to transmit his theories, and on the other hand travelled tirelessly within each state and among the feudal rulers, preaching and promoting his theories.

At the time, the states of Chu and Yue had engaged in naval warfare on the waters of the Yangzi River; Yue had utilized its topographical advantages to defeat Chu several times. After Gongshu Pan (that is, Lu Ban) had set off south towards Chu, he constructed for Chu a new type of weapon— a hooked halberd. Because of this, Chu routed Yue. In Mozi's presence Gongshu Pan boasted of the deadly efficiency of the hooked halberd, and satirized Mozi, saying, "In naval warfare my hooked halberd is able to defeat the enemy; I don't know whether your 'rightness' is able to do to the same?" Mozi said, " 'The hooked halberd of my rightness' is better than your hooked halberd by a hundred times. My hooked halberd has rightness at its core; it uses universal love for its 'hook' and veneration and respect for its 'blade.' Leading others to treat each other with mutual love and respect is the only way to gain advantage for all. Now you use hooks to block others, and others use hooks to block you; you use blades to repel others, and others use blades to repel you. Hooking and

民的疾苦。于是他很早便萌发出改变不合理现实、挽救天下苍生于水火的人生理想。他发奋学习，希望能从儒家的学说中寻觅出救世之道。但是孔子死后儒家分派，很多孔门弟子都陷入在"洒扫、应对、进退"这些繁琐的礼仪之中，而较少关心人民的生活。这些不顾民生的礼仪使墨子越来越反感，他开始意识到，仅靠这些烦扰的礼仪来拯救天下并不现实，而有了"礼仪倾扰而不悦，厚葬靡财而贫民，久服伤生而害事"❶这样的感叹。于是，他毅然背离儒家，创立了自己的学派——墨家。

创立墨家学派之后，墨子以"兴天下之利，除天下之害"❷为己任，为平民百姓的利益四处奔走，很快就获得了人民的信任。学派的规模迅速壮大，墨家学说的影响也日益深远。在那个风行招贤养士的年代，各国君主也都想借助墨子的力量为其服务。为了解万民于倒悬之苦，墨子一方面广招弟子传授自己的学说，另一方面则不辞疲倦地奔走于各国诸侯之间，四处游说。

当时，楚国曾与越国在长江上进行水战，越国利用有利地势，多次打败楚国。公输盘（即鲁班）从鲁国南游到楚国后，为楚国制造了新式兵器——钩镶，楚国因而大败越国。公输盘在墨子面前自夸钩镶的灵巧，并讽刺墨子说："在船战时我有钩镶可以击败敌人，不知你的'义'能否做到呢？"墨子说："我的'义的钩镶'比你的'钩镶'要好上百倍。我的'钩镶'以义为核心，用兼爱来'钩'，用恭敬来'镶'。使人们互相关爱、恭敬，才能互相得利。现在你用钩来阻止别人，别人也用钩来阻止你；你用镶来推开别人，别人也用镶来推开你。

---

❶《淮南子·要略》。
❷《兼爱下》。

[1] Huainanzi, "Yaolue."
[2] "Universal Love," Part Three.

blading each other leads to mutual destruction. What is there to boast of in your hooked halberd?"

Even though in this dialogue with Gongshu Pan Mozi utterly routed him and left him speechless, still it provoked a thought in Mozi, that is, he could not merely depend on crying "I oppose offensive warfare" with a loud voice without being able to check incursions; he must have a practical course of conduct to fend off unrighteous warfare. Therefore he led his disciples to expend a large amount of energy to research the theory of defensive warfare and to manufacture defensive weapons, and actively engaged in opposing wars of invasion. When he heard that Gongshu Pan once again manufactured scaling ladders to prepare to attack the state of Song, he immediately set off for Chu. On the way he ate and slept outdoors, and travelled for ten days and nights until at length he arrived in Ying, the capital of Chu (in the north of modern Jiangling city in Hubei).

When he saw Gongshu Pan, Mozi laid the issue right on the table: "Someone in the north is opposing me; you are my good friend and I want you to help me kill him." Upon hearing this, Gongshu Pan's face turned sour, looking displeased, but he did not make a sound. Seeing this, Mozi continued on speaking, saying, "Do not be unhappy. I am willing to offer you ten units of gold as your reward." Gongshu Pan looked enraged, and somberly stated, "I make a point of being just and right, and have never ever killed anyone." Mozi leaped into that opening to cut to his real theme, "Good! You try to be just and right, and do not kill innocent persons. But then why do you help Chu to manufacture scaling ladders to allow them to kill the innocent people of Song?" Gongshu Pan was immediately dumbfounded, and stayed so for a long time before he finally said, "What you say makes sense, but I have already promised the king of Chu, and cannot go back on my word!" Mozi said, "Fine, take me to see the king of Chu!"

"I have long heard of your name and fame, and they have resounded in my ear. This time you have traveled a long distance to come. Is there something you have to instruct me about?" asked the king of Chu when he saw Mozi.

"Please excuse my ignorance, but I have something for you to clarify, so I have made it a point to come see you, Great King, and ask you for instruction. There is a man now who has a beautiful chariot, but he has always wanted to steal the old broken down cart of his neighbor. He does own his own beautiful clothing but wants to steal the coarse and tattered clothing of his neighbor. He has his own delicacies to eat, yet still wants to steal the coarse grain eaten by his neighbor. What type of person would you call this man?" Mozi asked in a

彼此互相钩镶，就是互相残害。你这样的钩镶有什么值得夸耀的呢？"

此次对话虽然将公输盘驳斥得哑口无言，但也使墨子意识到，仅靠大声疾呼"非攻"并不能抑制住侵略，必须以实际行动来阻止不义之战。因此，他带领弟子花费大量精力研究防御理论和制作防御器械，积极从事抵抗侵略的战争。当他听说公输盘又为楚国制造了云梯准备攻打宋国时，便立即动身前往楚国。一路上风餐露宿，披星戴月，走了十天十夜，终于到达楚国的都城郢（今湖北江陵北）。

见到公输盘，墨子劈头一句就说："北方有人与我作对，你是我的好朋友，我想请你帮我杀了他。"公输盘听后脸色很不高兴，没有作声。墨子见此接着说道："您别不高兴，我愿意奉赠十镒黄金作为报酬。"公输盘面有怒色，严肃地说："我讲道义，从来不无故杀人。"墨子趁机将话题切入："好！你讲道义，不杀无辜之人。那为什么要帮助楚国制造云梯，让他们去杀害无辜的宋国人呢？"公输盘顿时哑口无言，愣了半天才说："你说的是有道理，可是我已经答应了楚王，不能出尔反尔啊！"墨子便道："那好，你带我去见见楚王吧！"

"久仰先生大名，如雷贯耳。此次远道而来，不知有何见教？"楚王见面就问墨子。

"请原谅我的愚昧，有一件事情我不明白，特地来向大王请教。现在有一个人，他自己家里有华丽的车子，却老想偷邻居家的破车。自己有华丽的衣服，却总想偷别人的粗布烂衫。自己家有山珍海味，却还想偷吃邻居家的粗食糟糠。这是一个

calm, unhurried manner.

"He should certainly be considered as having contracted a strange type of kleptomania," answered the king of Chu without stopping to think.

"Right! But I still do not understand: your large state is five thousand square *li* of territory, and possesses lakes and land capable of producing wonderful and precious animal life; but the state of Song is only five hundred *li* square, and it is hard to find even a pheasant or a rabbit. Isn't this just like the difference between embroidered brocade and coarse and tattered clothing? Such rarities of timber like camphor trees and nanmu trees are all present in your honorable state; but in the state of Song, not even trees of medium height grow. Isn't this exactly like the case of the beautiful chariot compared to the dilapidated cart? Well, you Great King are setting off to attack Song. So what is different between you and that man who contracted the illness of kleptomania? I privately regard your actions in this regard as not very intelligent; it can only harm justice and morality and lead to you being laughed at by the entire world."

The king of Chu had no response, but after thinking long and hard said, "Your words, sir, are correct. But Gongshu Pan has already constructed scaling ladders for me, so Song must be attacked."

"You think, Great King, that having Gongshu Pan's scaling ladders will allow you to be victorious in your attack against their cities? I am afraid that this is not necessarily true. If you do not believe this, then let Gongshu Pan and I show you," replied Mozi with a plan in mind.

Thereupon Mozi removed his sash to serve as the model of a moat and used pieces of wood to serve as models of defensive weapons, and play-acted the scenario of an attack with Gongshu Pan in front of the king of Chu. Nine times did Gongshu Pan change the strategy of attack, and nine times Mozi calmly responded. Gongshu Pan wracked his brains but ultimately could not overcome Mozi's defenses.

When the king of Chu saw this he was startled, and was about to ask Gongshu Pan the best course of action when Gongshu Pan suddenly raised his head and said fiercely to Mozi, "I know how to deal with you. It is just that I will not tell you now." Mozi knew what he was thinking, and sarcastically responded, saying, "I also know how you will deal with me, but I also will not tell you."

The king of Chu listened to this and was puzzled, and asked in a wondering tone, "What are you saying? How is it that I cannot understand you?"

什么样的人呢？"墨子不紧不慢地问。

"那他肯定是得了喜欢偷窃的怪病。"楚王不假思索地答道。

"对啊。可是我还是不明白：贵国地方五千里，有大片生产珍奇异兽的湖泊和土地；宋国只有方圆五百里，连山鸡野兔都很少见到，这不正像锦绣之衣与粗布烂衫吗？贵国像香樟、楠木之类的珍贵木材也都应有尽有，宋国连比较高大的树木都不生长，这不正像华丽的车子和破烂的车子一样吗？那么大王去攻打宋国，和那位得了偷窃怪病的人有什么两样呢？我私下认为您的这种做法不太明智，只会伤害道义，被天下人耻笑。"

楚王无言以对，想了半天，说："先生的话没有错，但是公输盘已经为我造好了云梯，宋国是非打不可了。"

"大王以为有了公输盘造的云梯就能攻城取胜了吗？恐怕不见得吧！不信我和公输盘演示给你看看。"墨子胸有成竹地说。

于是墨子解下腰带比作城池，用木片比作防守的器械，与公输盘在楚王面前比试起来。公输盘九次改变了攻城的方案，墨子九次沉着应对。绞尽了脑汁的公输盘，最后还是没有攻破墨子的防守。

楚王见此大惊，正准备问公输盘如何是好，不料想公输盘突然抬起头来，恶狠狠地对墨子说："我知道该怎么对付你，只是我现在不说罢了。"墨子心知其意，冷冷地回说："我也知道你会怎么对付我，我也不说。"

楚王在一旁听得很纳闷，诧异地问道："你们在说什么啊，寡人怎么听不懂呢？"

"What Gongshu Pan means is that he wants to kill me, and thinks that in this way Song cannot hold out. But I tell you Great King in all seriousness that I have already dispatched my disciple Qin Huali and others, 300 in all, who have already brought my anti-siege weapons to Song and stand battle ready waiting for you. So even if you kill me, you will not prevail," was Mozi's powerful response.

In the face of Mozi, who was both brave and wise, the king of Chu could not help but shake his head. "OK, I have decided not to attack Song." In this way Mozi prevented a battle from breaking out that was on the verge of happening.

In addition to this magnificent maneuver of preventing an attack on Song by Chu, it should be stated that Mozi prevented countless battles between states during the Warring States Period. According the account of the "Questions from Lu" section, in order to prevent warfare between Qi and Lu, Mozi travelled back and forth between the two states three times, persuading the lords and ministers of both states to withdraw their troops and end hostilities.

The first time was when the lord of Lu learned that the state of Qi was about to attack his own state; he asked Mozi whether he had a means of resolving the situation. Mozi felt that even if a state were small and its people poor, as long as it was able to hold loyal ministers close at hand and enact humaneness and fealty like Yu of Xia, Tang of Shang, and Kings Wen and Wu of Zhou, then it would be able to unite the world. Therefore Mozi urged the lord of Lu not to worry; as long as he venerated Heaven and served the spirits above, and below loved and benefited the commoners, prepared much money and wealth, talked humbly with the feudal lords on the periphery of the state to express his respect, united the commoners of the entire nation to work as one and to oppose the state of Qi in one body, then the danger could be dissipated, and worries would cease.

The second time was when the state of Qi was already armed and ready to go, warfare could break out at the slightest provocation. Mozi said to the lead general of Qi Xiangzi Niu, "Attacking Lu would be a grave mistake for Qi. Previously to the east King Fuchai of Wu attacked the state of Yue and forced King Goujian to retreat to Kuaiji; to the west he attacked Chu and forced King Zhao to flee to the state of Sui; to the north he attacked Qi and captured Guo Shu, the general of Qi. Later on the feudal states rose up en masse to take revenge. His subjects were exhausted from fleeing for their lives, and were no longer willing to serve him. As a result, his state was destroyed and he himself

"公输盘的意思，不过是想杀掉我，以为这样宋国就守不住了。但我实话告诉大王，我的弟子禽滑厘等三百人，已经带着我的守城器械在宋国严阵以待了。你们就是杀掉我，一样不会得逞！"墨子凛然答道。

面对智勇双全的墨子，楚王无可奈何地摇了摇头，"好吧，我决定不攻打宋国了。"一场迫在眉睫的战争就这样被墨子化解了。

除了这次止楚攻宋的壮举，墨子消弭各国战争的活动可以说不计其数。据《鲁问》篇记载，为了阻止齐鲁之间的战争，墨子曾辗转两国，前后三次游说两国的君臣止兵休战。

第一次，鲁君得知齐国将要攻打自己的国家，问墨子是否有解救的办法。墨子认为，即使国小民贫，只要能像夏禹、商汤、周文王和周武王一样亲近忠臣，推行仁义，就能一统天下。墨子因此劝说鲁君不必担心，只要上能尊天事鬼，下能爱利百姓，多准备钱财，用谦卑的言论向周边诸侯表示敬意，使全国的百姓齐心协力，共同对抗齐国，就可以化险为夷，解除忧患。

第二次，齐国已经整装待发，战争一触即发。墨子对齐国大将项子牛说："攻打鲁国，将会成为齐国犯的大错。从前，吴王夫差向东攻打越国，将越王勾践逼退到会稽；向西攻打楚国，迫使楚昭王逃到随国；向北攻打齐国，俘虏了齐国的将军国书。后来诸侯群起报仇，他的百姓疲于奔命，再不肯为他效力。结果国破家亡，自己也被杀死。智伯瑶攻打范氏与中行氏，

was killed, Zhi Boyao attacked the Fan clan and the Zhonghang clan, annexing the territory of the Three Jins. As a result the feudal lords rose up en masse and attacked him; ultimately his fate was the same as that of the state of Wu. Therefore when a great state attacks small states, it ends up in mutual destruction; this kind of aggression often is the path to self-destruction."

The third time was when Mozi personally called on Duke Tai of Qi. He asked him, saying, "Here is a knife, use it to try to behead someone; if you can do it in an instance should it be considered a sharp knife?" Duke Tai of Qi said, "Certainly it would be sharp." Mozi continued and said, "If you used this knife to cut off the heads of many persons, and it worked equally fast, would it be considered a sharp knife?" Duke Tai of Qi responded, "Of course it would be considered a sharp knife." Then Mozi asked again, "The knife tested out to be sharp, but who was punished for all of this?" Duke Tai of Qi said, "Those who tested the knife by beheading innocent persons should be punished." Mozi said, "Well then annexing other states, destroying the armies of other states, murdering innocent populations, who was punished for all of this?" Duke Tai of Qi thought deeply for a long while, then abruptly became enlightened and said, "I should be punished!"

Mozi was like an angel of peace descended among the people, and ran himself ragged his whole life for the sake of their peace and good fortune. Song, Wey, Chu, Qi, Yue and Wei all saw the numerous silhouettes of him industriously doing good. Among the people was current a saying that "Mozi never warmed up a mat," meaning that for the sake of doing good he did not even have enough time to sit down long enough to warm up a mat.

The great undertaking that Mozi performed as he sacrificed his life for the right caused him to be considered as a sage in the eyes of the common people. Not only did his followers increase more and more, the monarchs of each state also competed to show their respect for him. For instance, the king of Yue once agreed to confer a feudal territory on him of "five hundred square *li* of former Wu territory," and prepared fifty chariots to go to Lu to escort him. But Mozi said, "If the king of Yue is willing to give heed to my teaching and adopt my theories, then I will go; otherwise if I were to go, wouldn't it be betraying rightness? If I were to sell rightness, I can sell it to any state, why only sell to Yue?"

While in Chu, Mozi once presented a book to King Hui; King Hui called out in pleasure, "a fine book." ❶ He wanted to recruit Mozi, but Mozi absolutely refused because the king had not implemented his theories.

兼并三晋之地，结果诸侯群起而攻之，最终也和吴国的下场一样。所以大国攻打小国，那是互相残害，这种侵略往往是自取灭亡。"

第三次，墨子亲自参见齐太公，问道："现在这里有把刀，用它试砍人的头，一下子就砍了下来，可以称得上锋利吗？"齐太公说："的确锋利。"墨子接着说："假如用这把刀接连试砍许多人的头，都能随手而砍下来，可以称得上锋利吗？"齐太公答："当然算得上锋利了。"墨子又问："刀算是试出锋利了，但谁将因此受到惩罚呢？"齐太公说："试刀砍头的人无故杀人，他将遭到惩罚。"墨子说："那么兼并别的国家，消灭别国军队，残杀无辜百姓，谁将因此遭到惩罚呢？"齐太公沉思良久，猛然醒悟道："我将遭受惩罚啊！"

墨子就像一位降临人间的和平天使，为了人民的安宁幸福，一生辛劳奔波，宋、卫、楚、齐、越、魏等国家都留下了他孜孜行义的身影。人们有"墨子无暖席"的说法，说的就是墨子为了行义，甚至连坐暖席子的时间都没有。

墨子舍生取义的种种壮举使他成为当时平民眼中的"圣人"，不仅追随者越来越多，各国君主也纷纷向他表示敬意。如越王曾许诺封给墨子"故吴之地方五百里"，并准备了五十辆车到鲁国迎接墨子。墨子却说："如果越王能听从我的言论，采用我的学说，那我就去。否则我去了，岂不是把义给出卖了？要卖我卖给哪国都可以，何必非要卖给越国呢？"

在楚国，墨子曾向楚惠王献书，惠王看后惊呼"良书"❶，很想招纳墨子，可墨子却因为惠王没有施行他的学说决然而辞。

---

❶《渚宫旧事》。

❶ "Past Event at the Riverine Palace."

Mozi had numerous opportunities like this to serve as an official; but because the monarchs of the various states were not able to give heed to his words or implement his way, they were all resolutely rejected by Mozi. As a result, Mozi was on the go his entire life and never held any office. Although he enjoyed the honorary title of the "grandee from Lu," he had no experience in political office. With regard to his actions in rejecting salaried office for the sake of doing good, many persons of the time said that they could not understand him. One Confucian called Wumazi once asked Mozi in this fashion, "You travel all around doing good, but the people do not help you in this; neither do the ghosts nor spirits protect you because of this, but you still persist in your course. Can it be that you are crazy?" Mozi asked a question in reply, "Say, you employ two stewards; one of them would work when he saw you, but would not work when he did not see you; the other one would work when he saw you, and would still work even though he did not see you. Which one would you respect?" Wumazi said, "I would naturally respect the latter one." Mozi laughed and said, "Then aren't you respecting a crazy man?"

Because the world was under a cloud of darkness at the time, even Mozi's old friends urged him to stop doing good, why should one man persist in working so hard? But Mozi said, "One man had ten sons; if only one of them busied himself with the plowing and the others dithered away their time enjoying their leisure, well, the one who worked had to redouble his effort in plowing; this was because those who ate were many while those who planted the fields were few. Now the people in the world only worry about themselves. You should urge me to work even harder. How could you think of urging me to stop instead?"

Embracing a heart of utter goodness and sincerity, Mozi took upon himself the duty of saving the world his entire life, completely rejecting personal glory or shame. The noble spirit of "his clarion call that he did not do enough for the world," ❶ his self-rectification through a carpenter's chalk line, and his great character of tasking himself to the limits of his ability, not only are the backbone of the Chinese race, but also are the backbone of the human race and the backbone of the world.

像这样的做官机会还有很多，由于各国国君都不能够听其言、行其道，都被墨子断然拒绝了。结果，墨子奔波了一生，却终生未仕。虽有"宋之大夫"这一名誉头衔，终究没有为政的经历。对于这种背禄向义的做法，在当时就有许多人表示难以理解。一个名叫巫马子的儒士曾这样问墨子："您四处行义，人们并没有因此而帮助你，鬼神也没有因此而保佑你，但是您还坚持这么做，难道您疯了吗？"墨子反问道："如果你有两个家臣，其中一个见到你就做事，见不到你就不做事；另一个见到你就做事，见不到你也做事，你会器重谁？"巫马子说："我自然会器重后者。"墨子笑道："那你这不是也器重有疯病的人吗？"

因为当时天下昏昏，就连墨子的老朋友也都劝他不要再行义，何必一个人苦苦坚持？墨子却说："一个人有十个儿子，如果只有一个人忙于耕种而其他九个人都游手好闲，那么这个做事的儿子就不能不更加努力地耕种。因为吃饭的人多而种地的人少。现在天下人都只顾自己，你应该劝勉我尽力奔走，怎么反倒阻止我呢！"

怀着一颗至善至诚之心，墨子一生以救世为己任，全然抛弃了个人荣辱。其"昭昭然为天下忧不足"❶的可贵精神，以绳墨自矫、以自苦为极的伟大人格，不仅是中华民族的脊梁，也是人类的脊梁，天下的脊梁。

---

❶《荀子·富国》。

❶ *Xunzi*, "Enriching the State."

春秋时期的陶罐
A Pottery Jar of the Spring and Autumn Period

三　薪尽火传，后来居上
——墨家后学的派别及活动

Chapter Ⅲ　　The Torch of Learning is Passed Down, the New Generation Improves on the Old: Later Mohist Schools and Activities

After Mozi established the Mohist school, its influence expanded greatly; the disciples who followed him increased without ceasing. According to the *Spring and Autumn Annals of Mr. Lü*, "What Should be Dyed," "The followers of Confucius and Mozi increased all the more, and their disciples grew even more numerous, filling all the world." Following the great development of this school, the Mohists gradually formed a scholastic group with a strict organizational nature, a unified code of conduct and a unified economy.

The members of the Mohist school all adhered to the scholastic theories established by Mozi; they took as their belief the achievement of Mozi's social and political ideals; they wandered all around lecturing to the feudal princes, serving in office, and implementing Mozi's theories as their primary duty. Before these disciples served in office, Mozi often would first dispatch several renowned disciples to lecture and set the stage. For instance, before Gao Shizi went to the state of Wey to take up office, Mozi sent Guan Qian'ao to first go there to engage in propaganda work in order to elevate Gao Shizi's reputation.

After taking up office, the actions of the disciples would be controlled by the school; if their conduct went against the aims of the Mohists, then they would be dismissed. The section "Questions from Lu" recorded the story of Sheng Chuo being fired. Mozi's disciple Sheng Chuo served in office under Xiangzi Niu; three times Xiangzi Niu invaded the state of Lu, obviously violating Mozi's principle of "Opposing Offensive Warfare." Sheng Chuo not only did not dissuade him, but all three times accompanied Xianzi Niu on his incursions into Lu. After Mozi heard of this, he made Gao Sunzi force him to quit.

Opposite to this, because the ruler of the state of Wey was benighted and inhuman and would not enact the theories of Mohism, Gao Shizi resolutely abandoned his generous stipend and quit his office to return to his school. Mozi greatly praised his spirit of abandoning wealth for the sake of righteousness: "I have constantly heard of those who abandon the right way for the sake of high office and a large salary; of those who abandon high office and a large salary for the sake of the right way, other than Gao Shizi, who else is there?" Obviously, setting off to take up office was merely one ploy used to propagandize Mozi's theories. If this ploy was unable to be achieved, then members of the scholarly group would be duty-bound to abandon office.

The economic lives of the members were likewise controlled by their school. Mozi advocated "those with wealth should strive to share it with others." ❶ These sentiments were also directed towards members of the school.

墨子自创立墨家学派后，影响日益扩大，追随弟子也不断增多，据《吕氏春秋·当染》记载，孔墨"从属弥众，弟子弥丰，充满天下"。随着学派的发展壮大，墨家逐渐形成具有严密组织性、行动统一化、经济一体化的学术团体。

墨家学团的成员统一信奉墨子创立的学说，他们以实现墨子的社会政治理想为信仰，四处游说诸侯、出仕为官，推行墨子学说是他们的首要任务。在弟子出仕之前，墨子往往会先指派其他几名弟子前去游说铺垫。比如在高石子到卫国做官前，墨子就让管黔敖先到卫国进行宣传，以提高高石子的知名度。

弟子出仕后，他们的行为仍要受到学团的掌控，如果行事有悖于墨家主旨，就会被罢免。《鲁问》篇就记载了胜绰被辞退的故事：墨子的弟子胜绰在项子牛手下做官，而项子牛先后三次入侵鲁国，明显违背了墨子"非攻"的主张。胜绰不但没有劝阻，反而三次都跟随项子牛一起入侵鲁国。墨子听说后就让高孙子辞退了他。

与之相反，因为卫国国君昏庸无道、不施行墨家学说，高石子毅然舍弃优厚的待遇，辞官回到学团。对于他这种背禄向义的精神，墨子大加赞赏："我经常听说为了高官厚禄而背弃道义的人，为了道义而舍弃高官厚禄的人，除了高石子还能有谁啊！"很显然，出仕为官只是学团宣传墨子学说的一种手段，如果这种手段无法奏效，学团成员就要义不容辞地舍弃它。

成员的经济生活同样也受到学团的控制。墨子主张"有财者勉以分人"[1]，对学团内部的成员也是如此。据《耕柱》篇

---

[1] 《尚贤下》。

[1] "Elevating the Worthy," Part Three.

According to what is recorded in the section "Geng Zhu," after Geng Zhuzi was recommended by Mozi to go to the state of Chu to be an official, several of his fellow students went to visit him. For each meal he only served them three liters of rice, obviously a very shabby meal. The classmates said to Mozi after their return, "Geng Zhuzi in Chu serves no purpose." But Mozi said, "You cannot make such a conclusion!" It turns out that not long afterwards, Geng Zhuzi sent ten catties of gold to Mozi, saying, "Your student is unworthy, but I have gathered ten catties of gold; please, Master, share this with everyone." From this we can see that, regardless of which member was abroad earning income, they all would turn it over to the school, and then the leader would make a unified distribution for its utilization. Actually, this was a kind of unified economic system.

This strict management method and standardized organizational format insured that the Mohist school enjoyed a strong vitality during that chaotic and fragmented age. The influence of Mohism rapidly expanded, becoming the only school able to compete with the Confucians in the later part of the Warring States Period.

While Mozi was still alive, he led his school to reach it apogee based on his own erudition and his own lofty character. After he passed away, how could such a large school continue to maintain its cohesiveness?

We already know that Mohism was not simply a scholarly school or an academic organization; it was also a tightly organized social group. The chief leader of the Mohists had his special designation, called a "grandmaster." Within the Mohist organization the grandmaster enjoyed ultimate authority and prestige. All members of the Mohist organization had to obey the orders of the master.

The Chinese words meaning master individually meant "great" and "master," so the term actually meant "grand teacher" or "grandmaster." The first generation leader of the Mohists was the founder of Mohism Mo Di; but what is worth noting is that he was only called Mozi or Master Mozi but was not called "grandmaster." It is evident that at that time this designation had not yet been coined. From this we may be sure that the title of grandmaster did not appear until after Mozi, and it was created to strengthen the authority of the leader.

Among extant pre-Qin works, only the *Spring and Autumn Annals of Mr. Lü* preserves any events related to the grandmaster; one records the names of three of them: Meng Sheng, Tian Xiangzi and Fu Tun. But no historical materials indicate that the most famous disciple of Mozi, Qin Huali, was a

记载：耕柱子被墨子举荐到楚国做官后，几个同门前去拜访他。耕柱子每顿饭只用三升米来招待他们，显得非常寒酸。同门回来后就对墨子说："耕柱子在楚国没有什么用处。"墨子却说："还不能这样下定论啊！"果然，没过多久，耕柱子就送了十斤黄金给墨子，并说："弟子不才，收入了十斤黄金，请老师和大家享用。"由此可见，无论哪位成员在外有了收入，都要上缴学团，再由首领统一分配使用。实际上这是一种一体化的经济制度。

严密的管理方法和规范的组织形式使墨家学团在那个动荡混乱、一盘散沙的时代显示出极其强大的生命力。墨家影响迅速扩大，成为战国中后期唯一可与儒家相抗衡的学派。

墨子在世时，他凭借自己渊博的学识和崇高的人格带领墨家学派达到鼎盛。墨子去世后，庞大的墨家学团又是如何继续维系其凝聚力的呢？

我们已经知道，墨家不单纯是一个学派或学术团体，它同时也是一个有着严密组织性的社会团体。墨家首领有其特殊的称号，叫做"巨子"。巨子在墨家组织内部拥有至高无上的权力和权威，墨家的全体成员都必须完全听命于巨子。

"巨"在中国古代有"大"的含义，"巨子"即为"大师"、"大先生"之义。墨家的第一代领袖是墨学的创立者墨翟，但值得注意的是，墨子却不是墨家第一位巨子。纵观《墨子》全书，对墨子的称呼只有"墨子"、"子墨子"，而没有"巨子"，

grandmaster of Mohism. In the work *Mozi* there occasionally is a mention of a "Master Qinzi." From this we may extrapolate that even if Mozi appointed Qin Huali as the head of the Mohists upon his deathbed, at that time the title of "grandmaster" still had not appeared. It was only when Qin Huali handed over his position to Meng Sheng did the title "grandmaster" start to appear. It is also possible that Qin Huali died before Mozi; we have no way of knowing. According to research, Meng Sheng and Wu Qi were contemporaries, and Mozi was senior to Wu Qi by more than 50 years, so it was entirely possible that Meng Sheng was Mozi's direct disciple at one remove. If Qin Huali died before Mozi, then the leader designated by Mozi upon his death should have been Meng Sheng. He then was the first grandmaster of the Mohists.

According to the *Spring and Autumn Annals of Mr. Lü*, "Supreme Virtue," Meng Sheng was on extremely friendly terms with the lord of Yangcheng of the state of Chu. This lord invited Meng Sheng to help him protect his own fiefdom, and he broke off a half-circle jade ring to serve as a tally. Both sides agreed that only when the two halves of the tally matched would the other obey the orders sent by a messenger to the other. Because the reforms of Wu Qi damaged the interests of the Chu aristocracy, when King Dao of Chu died, the Chu aristocracy including the lord of Yangcheng rose up in one body and besieged Wu Qi at the mourning site for King Dao. When shooting Wu Qi to death, they also shot arrows into the king's corpse by mistake. After King Su of Chu assumed the throne, he wanted to punish the crime of the one who had mistakenly shot the king's corpse. All that the lord of Yangcheng could do was to flee, so the state of Chu wanted to resume ownership of his fiefdom. At that time, Meng Sheng was still staying at Yangcheng defending the fiefdom of the lord of Yangcheng. Upon learning that Yangcheng was about to change hands, he said, "I received the fiefdom of the lord of Yangcheng as a charge, and have an agreement with him to use a tally. Now I have not seen his half of the tally, nor is my power sufficient to prevent his fiefdom from changing hands; all I can do is to offer up my life." His student Xu Ruo counseled him, saying, "Your death would not benefit the lord of Yangcheng in any way; moreover it would also destroy the power of the Mohists, so you absolutely cannot die!" But Meng Sheng rejected him, replying, "You are wrong; concerning the lord of Yangcheng, I am either his teacher or his friend, either his friend or the subject. If I do not die today, from

可见当时还无"巨子"之称。由此确定,巨子制应出现在墨子之后,是墨家后学为了强调领袖的权威所创。

现存先秦典籍中只有《吕氏春秋》中记载有巨子的事迹,其中载有巨子三人:孟胜、田襄子和腹䵍。而没有史料表明墨子最著名的大弟子禽滑厘是墨家的巨子,《墨子》一书中也只是偶尔称其为"子禽子"。由此推论虽然墨子在临终前指定禽滑厘为墨家首领,但那时还没有兴起"巨子"一称,直到禽滑厘传位给孟胜时才开始有"巨子"的称呼;抑或禽滑厘先于墨子去世也未可知。据考证,孟胜与吴起同时,而墨子比吴起年长五十余岁,孟胜极有可能是墨子的再传弟子。如果禽滑厘先于墨子而亡,那么墨子临终前指定的那位墨家首领应当是孟胜,他便是墨家的首任巨子。

据《吕氏春秋·上德》记载:孟胜与楚国的阳城君十分友好,阳城君请孟胜帮他守卫自己的封地,并剖开一块璜玉作为符信,双方约定只有合符才能听从来人所传达的命令。由于吴起的改革损害了楚国贵族的利益,楚悼王刚死,包括阳城君在内的楚贵族群起围攻吴起于悼王停丧处,在射杀吴起时也误射了王尸。楚肃王继位,要治误射王尸诸人的罪,阳城君只好出逃,楚国便要收回他的封地。当时孟胜还在留守阳城君的封地,得知封地将要被收回,他说:"我接受了阳城君的封地,并与他有符信约定,现在没有见到符信,自己的力量又无法制止封地被收回,我只能为此一死了。"他的学生徐若劝他:"你死了对阳城君毫无益处,而且还会使墨家力量灭绝,你万万不能死啊。"孟胜回绝道:"不对。对于阳城君而言,我不是老师就是

now on, those who seek out a strict teacher will certainly never look among us Mohists again; those who seek out a friend will certainly never look among us Mohists again; those who seek out a fine minister will certainly never look among us Mohists again. My death is precisely for the sake of insuring the enactment of the principles of Mohism and to insure the continuation of our mission! I will transmit the office of grandmaster to Tian Xiangzi of the state of Song; he is a worthy scholar, therefore I am not afraid that Mohism will be destroyed because of my death." After hearing this, Xu Ruo immediately decided to precede Meng Sheng in death. After Meng Sheng sent two disciples to give the office of grandmaster to Tian Xiangzi, he resolutely committed suicide, and was buried with Meng Sheng and 180 noted followers of Mohism. The two Mohists who had transmitted the office of grandmaster to Tian Xiangzi would not listen to what Tian Xiangzi urged them to do, but returned to the city of Yangcheng of the state of Chu and martyred themselves for the sake of Meng Sheng.

Superficially, this soul-stirring and tragic act seemed to put into practice the virtues taught by Mohists; the heroic deaths of Meng Sheng and his disciples, dying for their righteous cause, truly was Mohist in style. But a close analysis reveals that their so-called "righteous cause" actually ran counter to Mozi's righteous principle of "increasing the benefits in the world and eliminating harm." In the section "Questions from Lu," Mozi had already debated with Meng Shan concerning how to distinguish between righteousness and unrighteousness. Meng Shan said, "Previously, when Bai Gongsheng rebelled, he seized the Prince Zilü and grabbed a large ax and pressed it against his waist, and pointed the blade of a spear at his heart, and said to him, 'If you are willing to become the king of Chu, then I am willing to spare your life; if you are not willing, then I will kill you.' Zilü said, 'What a great insult to me! You kill my relatives, and then try to please me by offering me the Chu throne. Even if I were to gain the whole world, if I gained it by leaving the way of humaneness and fealty, then I would not do it, let alone merely for the Chu throne.' Therefore he resolutely refused to go along. Are you trying to say that Zilü is not to be considered humane and righteous?" Mozi's reply to this was, "This was truly hard to do, but it should not be considered as humane and righteous. If you consider that the king of Chu was inhumane, then why not accept the throne and govern Chu? If you think that Bai Gongsheng was unrighteous, then why not accept the throne, and then kill him and return the throne to the king of Chu?"

Obviously, Mozi did not distinguish between righteousness and

朋友，不是朋友就是臣子。如果我今天不死，从今以后，寻求严师一定不会从墨家中寻求了，寻找朋友一定不会从墨家中寻找了，寻觅良臣一定不会从墨家中寻觅了。我死，正是为了实践墨家的准则并使它的事业继续下去啊！我将传巨子之位给宋国的田襄子，他是位贤士，所以不用担心墨家因我之死而灭绝。"徐若听后当即决定先孟胜而死。孟胜则在派了两个弟子把巨子一位传给田襄子后便毅然自尽，和孟胜一起殉死的还有一百八十名墨家子弟。而那两位传达命令给田襄子的墨者也不听田襄子的劝说，返回楚国阳城为孟胜殉死了。

这么一场惊心动魄、可歌可泣的悲壮之举表面看来似乎行了墨家的大义，孟胜及其弟子慷慨赴死，殉身就义，确实颇具墨子之风。但仔细分析便可发现，他们这样的"义"举，却恰恰违背了墨子"为天下兴利除害"的大义准则。在《鲁问》篇中，墨子曾就如何区别义与不义与孟山进行过一番辨析。孟山说："从前白公胜叛乱，抓住王子间并用大斧抵着他的腰，用剑矛直对着他的心脏，对他说：'你愿意当楚王的话就让你活命，不愿意就让你死。'王子间说：'这是何等的侮辱我啊！杀死我的亲人，却拿楚国的王位来让我开心。即使我将得到整个天下，如果不合仁义之道，我也不会做，更何况只有楚国呢！'于是坚决不从。王子间难道不算仁义吗？"对此，墨子的回答是："这的确是很难做到的，但还称不上仁义。如果是认为楚王无道，为什么不接受王位并治理楚国呢？如果是认为白公胜不义，为什么不接收王位，然后再杀掉白公胜后把王位还给楚王呢？"

很显然，墨子并不是从个人恩怨私利出发来区别义与不义、

unrighteousness, whether or not one followed the Way on the basis of personal grudges or debts of gratitude. Yet given his personal belief that "a gentleman will die for his bosom friend," Meng Sheng misinterpreted Mozi's aim of "stimulating the benefits of the world, eliminating the harm in the world," taking it instead as the blind service of one family or clan. What is tragic is that his 180 and more disciples all felt that same way about this, and under his leadership strode out along the road of blind service. This kind of senseless sacrifice greatly harmed the vitality of Mohism, diminishing each day their influence during the later Warring States Period.

In addition to lamenting over all of this, we cannot help but wonder: after all what was the power to make 180 plus disciples follow Meng Sheng without regret in dying for their cause? Although there was an old saying that "When a lord wanted his minister to die, he would have no choice but to die; when a father wanted his son to perish, he would have no choice but to perish." But this type of relationship and duty did not exist between master and disciple. Furthermore, if a minister or son had to die, it was not something that they were happy to do. The phrase "cannot help but..." thus betrays the fact that they had no other choice.

Nevertheless, in the matter of the suicide of Meng Sheng, even if the two disciples who delivered the letter insisted on returning to Luyang to commit suicide, we can still see that the suicide of the 180 and more disciples was likewise of their own volition. If it was only a matter of obeying the summons of the grandmaster and following the rules of the Mohists, it is likely that it would have been difficult to make this many disciples willingly cast aside their own precious lives. From this we may infer that during the administration of Meng Sheng as the grandmaster, the Mohist school had already started to manifest a religious tendency. Guo Moruo once mentioned the following in reference to this, that the religious aura of the Mohists was very thick, and the grandmaster "probably was the equivalent of a religious patriarch of later ages." ❶ That is to say, the leader of the Mohists of this period already possessed the nature of a religious leader, and possessed the ultimate authority to decide all matters. During the age of Mozi, some disciples doubted Mozi's theories, yet by the time of Meng Sheng, the grandmaster had already become the consummate exemplar and the personification of the truth; his veracity could not be doubted.

Given the unique position of the grandmaster, how was it created? Mozi had advocated abdication, and the creation of the grandmaster of the Mohists also adhered to the system of abdication, that is, the grandmaster was selected

有道与无道的。然而孟胜却在"士为知己者死"的个人信念下，将墨子"兴天下之利，除天下之害"的宗旨，曲解为效力于一家一姓的愚忠。可悲的是，他的一百八十余位弟子对此却毫无异议，也在他的带领之下走上了愚忠之路。这种无谓的牺牲大大损失了墨家的有生力量，使墨家在战国中后期的影响日渐衰弱。

扼腕叹息之余，我们不禁又有疑惑：究竟是什么力量，能让一百八十余弟子无怨无悔地随同孟胜自杀殉义呢？虽说中国古时有"君要臣死，臣不能不死；父要子亡，子不能不亡"之说，但师徒之间是不存在这样的关系与义务的。况且臣与子受命而死也并非自身乐意而为，一句"不能不"也就流露出了他们不得已而为之的无奈。

然而，在孟胜殉节事件中，即使是传信的那两位弟子，仍执意要再返回鲁阳自杀，可见这一百八十余弟子的自杀皆为自愿。如果仅靠巨子的感召和墨家之法，恐怕很难使如此众多的弟子心甘情愿地抛却自己最宝贵的生命。由此可以推论，在孟胜为巨子的时代，墨家团体已经开始出现准宗教倾向。郭沫若就曾说过，墨家的宗教气味极浓，巨子"大概等于后世宗教的教祖"[1]。也就是说，这时的墨家领袖已兼具有宗教首领的性质，有着至高无上的权力，决定墨家组织的一切。在墨子时代，还有弟子置疑墨子的学说，然而到了孟胜时代，巨子已成为完美的代表，真理的化身，他的正确性已不容置疑。

巨子地位如此特殊，他们又是如何产生的呢？墨家鼓吹禅让，墨家巨子的产生也都遵循禅让制，即由前任巨子选定继任

---

[1] 郭沫若：《青铜时代》，中国人民大学出版社，2005年，第130页。

[1] Guo Moruo, *The Bronze Age*, Chinese People's University Press, 2005, p. 130.

by the previous grandmaster, who yielded his position when he was at the point of death. The selection of the grandmaster was entirely the decision of the last grandmaster; this type of organizational style embodied a great, hidden flaw for later Mohists. Since the newly appointed grandmaster had not been produced by the collective voice of all the Mohists, once a newly appointed grandmaster lacked leadership talent or personal charisma, then it would be hard for him to maintain the cohesiveness of such a large organization. Before the death of Meng Sheng, he hurriedly yielded his position to the next grandmaster Tian Xiangzi. Historical records concerning his acts are quite rare, so we may deduce that his influence was not very great. Nevertheless, when Mohism was flourishing, when Mohism was growing stronger every day, and when the traces of the followers of Mohism were left all over the country, it was hard for the leader Xiangzi, who was lacking in charisma, to maintain the unity of the Mohists. From this point on Mohism began to fragment.

Once Zhuangzi commented on the fragmentation that the Mohists had gone through. *Zhuangzi*, "The World," said, "The disciples of Xiangli Qin, the followers of Wu Hou, the Mohists from the south such as ku Huo, Yi Chi and Denglingzi all chanted the 'Mohist Canon,' yet their opinions were opposite to each other, so they were regarded as unorthodox Mohist sects." According to the investigation of Mr. Qian Mu, in ancient works the surname Wu of Wu Zixu was written like the Wu in "Five." Wu Zixu was a man from Chu during the Spring and Autumn Period. His descendants lived in the state of Qi. The followers of Wu Hou probably referred to the eastern Mohists who were active in one stretch of territory in the state of Qi. Mohism rose in the states of Song and Lu. The eastern Mohists had directly inherited the mantle of Mozi. In addition to this, the state of Qi advocated intellectual freedom. Therefore, the eastern Mohists were extremely active. But Ku Huo, Yi Chi, Denglingzi, et al., were called southern Mohists; they should be regarded as Mohists active in the region of Chu. During Mozi's lifetime, he went to Chu numerous times with his disciples. Late in life he stayed in Luyang in the state of Chu. Chu then was the last center of activity for Mozi, so the Mohists in the south final started flourishing because of this. The followers of Wu Hou were the disciples of Xiangli Qin. This means that Xiangli Qin definitely lived before the Mohists of the east had been formed. According to Mr. Qian Mu's investigations into historical gazetteers, the ancestral homeland of the Xiangli clan was in Fenyang of modern Shanxi. From this we may infer that Xiangli Qin was mostly likely a western Mohist who was active in the state of Qin.

Zhuangzi's discussion of different Mohist sects did not include the

者，并于临终前传位于他。巨子的选择完全决定于前任巨子，这样的组织方式给墨家留下了巨大的隐患。由于不是墨家全体成员共同推举产生，新任巨子一旦不具备领袖的才能和号召力，就很难使规模庞大的团体真正凝聚在一起。孟胜临终前匆匆传位的下一任巨子田襄子，历史上所有事迹记载甚少，可以推想当时他的影响并不是很大。然而在墨学兴盛，墨家团体日益壮大，墨徒足迹遍布全国的情况下，缺乏号召力的田襄子就很难维系墨家的统一，天下墨者由此开始分化。

庄子曾对墨家的分化现象作过讨论。《庄子·天下》说："相里勤之弟子，五侯之徒，南方之墨者苦获、已齿、邓陵子之属，俱诵《墨经》，而倍谲不同，相谓别墨。"据钱穆先生考证，古书中伍子胥的伍姓多作"五"。伍子胥是春秋时期楚国人，他有后人在齐国生活的，五侯之徒大概是指在齐国一带活动的东方墨者。墨学兴起于宋、鲁，东方墨者直接受承墨子衣钵，加之齐国倡导学术自由，因此东方之墨极为活跃。而苦获、已齿、邓陵子等被称作南方之墨，他们应当是活跃在楚地的墨者。墨子生前就曾多次与弟子前往楚国，晚年又客居楚之鲁阳，楚国是墨子最后的活动中心，南方之墨由此卒盛。五侯之徒是相里勤的弟子，那么相里勤必定是在东方之墨形成之前。据钱穆先生地方志考证，相里氏的祖居在今山西汾阳，由此推论相里勤大概就是当时活跃在秦国的西方墨者。

庄子所谈的墨家派别并不包括西方之墨，这大概与他生活

western Mohists. This was probably related to the fact that his home was rather distant from Qin and he did not understand the Mohists in Qin. Actually, the strongest Mohist sect of the time was the western Mohists. According to the account of the *Spring and Autumn Annals of Mr. Lü*, "Ridding What is Private," the grandmaster Fu Tun lived in the state of Qin. Fu Tun's son killed someone, so according to the laws of Qin he should have been put to death. At the time, King Hui of Qin took into account Fu Tun's great age, and the fact that he only had this one son, so he commuted his son's death sentence. But Fu Tun insisted on executing his only son in accordance with the Mohist doctrine of "those who kill others must die; those who injure others must be punished." Fu Tun's rigid adherence to Mohist law with no effort at favoritism truly attracted wide admiration, and this incident let King Hui display his lenient side in a state that had hitherto always rigidly applied the law. From this it is evident that the position and influence of Fu Tun was uncommon, and let us imagine the actual power of the Mohists in the state of Qin at the time. This was probably the reason that Tian Xiangzi who lived in the far-off state of Song transmitted his position to Fu Tun, who was in the distant state of Qin.

While Mozi was alive, he never went to Qin. The state of Qin at that time had never seen any activity by the Mohists. In addition to the fact that Qin was a remote and distant state of Rong barbarians where transportation was difficult, it indulged in wars of annexation that greatly conflicted with Mozi's advocacy of being "against offensive warfare." Well, why did later Mohists from each region rush to Qin? This was largely related to King Hui of Qin's policy of employing outsiders as ministers.

Mozi's advocacy of "honoring the worthy" clearly indicated the need for "not avoiding the poor and base," and for "not avoiding the closely and distantly related." In employing the worthy and talented one must "elevate them with rank, lavishly endow them with remuneration, employ them with duties, limit them with orders." ❶ As for those who are capable, one must "elevate and recommend them, enrich and ennoble them and make them high officials." As for those who were incapable, one must "repress and dismiss them, impoverish and debase them, and make them serve compulsory service." ❷ No matter one's background, as long as one was talented and capable, he would be able to find a place to display his own talents in the state of Qin. Among the seven powerful states during the Warring States Period, only Qin was able to truly achieve this. Added to this was the fact that Qin grew stronger day by day, so Qin was much more attractive to worthy men than any other state. This caused many scholars from beyond the borders of Qin to flood

的地方距秦国较远、对秦国墨者不太了解有关。其实，当时势力最盛的当属西方之墨。据《吕氏春秋·去私》记载，墨家巨子腹䵍就居住在秦国。腹䵍的儿子杀了人，依秦法当处以死刑。当时秦国的国君秦惠王顾及腹年事已高，又只有这么一个儿子，就赦免了他儿子的死罪。但是腹䵍却依据"杀人者死，伤人者刑"的墨者之法执意处死自己唯一的儿子。腹䵍严守墨者之法，毫不徇私之举着实令人敬佩，而在一向重法的秦国，仅因腹䵍之故就使秦惠王网开一面，可见腹䵍在秦国的地位和影响非同一般，也可以想象到墨家当时在秦国所具的实力。这恐怕也是身处宋国的田襄子要把巨子之位传给远在秦国的腹䵍的原因。

墨子在世时并没有到过秦国，当时的秦国也未见有墨者活动。除了秦远僻西戎之地、交通不便外，秦国大肆从事兼并战争的行径也与墨子"非攻"的主张有很大冲突。那么，为什么在墨子之后各地墨者却纷纷涌入秦国呢？这与秦惠王时期实行的客卿制有很大关系。

墨子主张"尚贤"，曾明确提出举贤要"不辟贫贱"、"不辟亲疏"；任用贤才要"高予之爵，重予之禄，任之以事，断予之令" ❶。对有能者要"举而上之，富而贵之，以为官长"、对无能者则要"抑而废之、贫而贱之，以为徒役" ❷。不管出身如何，只要有才能，都能在秦国找到施展自己才华的一方天地。战国七雄中只有秦国真正做到了这一点。再加上秦国国势日益强盛，秦国对天下贤人有着其他国家无可比拟的巨大吸引

---

❶ 《尚贤上》。
❷ 《尚贤中》。
❶ "Elevating the Worthy," Part One.
❷ "Elevating the Worthy," Part Two.

into the state, and Mohists also competed with each other to move to Qin. In addition, the state of Qin of the time not only stressed defensive warfare against minority peoples of the north, it also had to defend itself from the other six states while invading others among the six states. All of this caused Mohists' siege warfare defensive techniques to take on a huge military application.

In addition to Fu Tun, historical materials also recorded three other Mohists: Tian Jiu, Tang Guguo and Xiezi, who were active in Qin. The *Spring and Autumn Annals of Mr. Lü*, "The Beginning of the Season," recorded that Tian Jiu once had lived in Qin for three years, but the *Spring and Autumn Annals of Mr. Lü*, "Eliminating Pardons," also recorded that an eastern Mohist called Xiezi desired to head west to Qin to have an audience with King Hui; King Hui asked Tang Guguo what his opinion was. Tang Guguo was concerned that Xiezi's learning and talents were higher than his own, so he vilified Xizi for being evil, blocking Xiezi from being able to see King Hui. From this incident we can see that the "eastern Mohists" and the "Qin Mohists" had already divided into different groups. Therefore, by the time of King Hui of Qin at the latest, Mohists had already developed a branch of Qin Mohists in the west. By the time of Zhuangzi, eastern Mohists, western Mohists and southern Mohists had already helped form a tripart divison of power within Mohism.

Following along with the further development of Mohism, the distribution of the followers of Mohism scattered wider and wider day by day, leading to an increasingly fragmented situation. The *Han Feizi*, "Display Learning," said, "Since the death of Mozi, there were the Mohists of the Xiangli clan, the Mohists of the Xiangfu clan and Mohists of the Dengling clan. Hence after Confucius and Mozi, Confucians split into eight sects, Mohists divided into three, what they accepted and rejected were opposite, yet all claimed to be the true inheritors of Confucius or Mozi." The Mohists of the Dengling clan doubtlessly were the southern Mohists. And "the Xiangli clan Mohists" were what Zhuangzi described as the "Disciples of Xiangli Qin and the followers of Wu Hou", i.e. eastern Mohists. As for the Mohists of the Xiangfu clan, Zhuangzi did not mention them; they probably were a sect that had not yet been formed at this time; the time that they were formed should then be later than the followers of Wu Hou and Deng Lingzi's subordinates.

From this we can see that each sect among the later followers of Mozi did not come into being at the same time. Even though all of them enjoyed a certain relationship due to historical transmission, their appearance demonstrated that Mohist schools of disciples no longer were divided into the

力，使得许多秦国以外的士人纷纷来奔，墨家之徒也争相涌入秦国。另外，当时的秦国不仅注重对北方少数民族的防御，而且在进攻六国的同时也要防止六国的进攻，这些都使墨家的守城之术有了巨大的用武之地。

除了腹䵍，史料记载还有三位墨者：田鸠、唐姑果和谢子，曾活动于秦国。《吕氏春秋·首时》中记载田鸠曾在秦国居住过三年。而《吕氏春秋·去宥》也记载：一位名叫谢子的东方之墨想西去秦国拜见秦惠王，惠王询问唐姑果的意见，唐姑果担心谢子的才学高过自己，就诋毁谢子为人险恶，致使谢子无法得到惠王召见。从这件事也可看出，在当时"东方之墨"与"秦墨"已分属不同集团。因此，最晚在秦惠王时期，墨家已分裂出西方秦墨一派。到了庄子时代，东方之墨、西方之墨与南方之墨已呈现出三足鼎立之势。

随着墨学的进一步发展，墨徒所居范围日益分散，致使墨家分化现象愈来愈严重。《韩非子·显学》中说："自墨子之死也，有相里氏之墨，有相夫氏之墨，有邓陵氏之墨。故孔墨之后，儒分为八，墨离为三，取舍相反不同，而皆自谓真孔墨。"邓陵氏之墨无疑就是南方之墨了。而"相里氏之墨"即庄子所说的"相里勤之弟子五侯之徒"的东方之墨。至于相夫氏之墨，庄子并没有论及，大概此时这一派还未形成，其形成时间应当晚于五侯之徒和邓陵子之属。

由此可见，墨家后学各派并非同时形成，虽然彼此间有着一定的师承关系，他们的出现表明墨家不再以"谈辩"、"说书"和"从事"为标准来区分弟子派别，取而代之的是按地域划分

debaters, commentators and doers. What replaced this method of division were different sects on the basis of regional divisions. This was due to the division of regions during the Warring States Period by feudal princes. On the basis of the political environments and human culture and geography differing in each region, in the course of development Mohism was molded and influenced by different cultures. Following the passage of time, the difference in intellectual theories and styles of conduct by Mohists in different regions became more and more acute, and more and more divergences occurred. After a time, different sects naturally were formed.

In addition to this, the competition for seizing the position of grandmaster was an important reason for the fragmentation of Mohism. In discussing the phenomenon of the fragmentation of the Mohist school, Zhuangzi said that each sect of Mohists "regarded the grandmaster as a saint, and were all willing to be his 'representative,' hoping to become his posterity; up to the present time this issue has not been decided." ❶ In the pre-Qin period "representative" in general indicated an ancestor. During a sacrifice, a member of a class lower than the ancestor or an old man would dress up in the image of the one being sacrificed to; this then was the "representative." From this we can see that during the time of Zhuangzi the Mohists had no grandmaster; therefore, the old position of grandmaster became the object of sacrifice on the part of Mohists. And grandmaster Fu Tun was only a little earlier than Zhuangzi, so it was entirely possible that the last grandmaster was Fu Tun, or was somebody who had died before Zhuangzi and had received his office from Fu Tun. Perhaps sudden death had caused the last grandmaster to be unable to designate his successor, or perhaps it was some other reason for the loss of this office among the Mohists. With the group of Mohists lacking a leader, each regional leader would want to become the next grandmaster; the struggle would have grown more and more fierce, leading to the ceaseless fragmentation of Mohists.

Mohism was born in the state of Lu and flourished in Song, and then shifted to Chu; ultimately it moved westward to Qin. In these various regions different Mohist sects were formed. Although each sect called the other sects "different Mohists," and each struggled to be considered orthodox, such internal debates and criticisms did not impact the progress and development of Mohism. The meticulous summaries of Mozi's theories on the part of the disciples of the school kept infusing fresh blood into Mohism, ultimately forming the book of *Mozi*.

的不同派别。这是因为战国时期诸侯地域割据，由于各地的政治环境和人文地理不尽相同，墨学在发展过程中受到不同文化的熏陶和影响。随着时间的推移，不同地域的墨家在学术主张和行事作风等方面的差别越来越大，分歧也越来越多，久而久之，自然会形成不同的派别。

除此之外，争夺巨子之位也是墨家分化的重要原因。庄子在论述墨家分化现象时曾说墨家各派"以巨子为圣人，皆愿为之尸，冀得为其后世，至今不决" ❶。在先秦时期，"尸"一般是指祖先。祭祀时，由被祭者的下级或晚辈装扮成被祭者的神像，这就是"尸"。由此可见，庄子时墨家已无巨子，因此，旧有巨子就成为墨者们祭祀的对象。而巨子腹䵍只是略早于庄子，那么墨家最后一位巨子很有可能就是腹䵍，或者是先于庄子而卒的腹䵍的继任者。也许是猝死使最后一位巨子没来得及指定自己的接班人，也许是别的什么原因，墨家巨子之位失传了。墨家集团一时群龙无首，各地墨者首领都想成为下一任巨子，斗争愈演愈烈，导致墨家不断分化。

墨学发于鲁、兴于宋，然后转移到楚，最后西移至秦，在不同区域形成了不同墨家流派。虽然各派之间互谓"别墨"、互争正宗，但彼此的辩诘和驳难并未影响墨学的演进与发展。由这些墨家弟子精心总结的墨子学说，不断地给墨学注入新鲜血液，最终成就了《墨子》一书。

---

❶《庄子·天下》。
❶ Zhuangzi, "The World."

《墨子》书影

Picture of the *Mozi*

四 包罗万象，独树一帜

——墨家的主要著作

Chapter Ⅳ   All-Embracing Learning, a Unique School of Thought: The Major Works of Mohism

Very few Mohist works have been transmitted; the most famous is the book of *Mozi*. Although this work is ascribed to Mo Di, the true author was not Mozi himself. Ancient books in the pre-Qin period, especially works by the various philosophers, were mostly the thinking and theories of the master collected and edited by his disciples, which gradually were edited and finalized. The process of book formation often required several generations of disciples, and the span could reach the space of a hundred years. Hence *Mozi* was the crystallization of the collective wisdom of Mozi's disciples and later followers. The work not only recorded Mozi's major theories and thought, it also included the development and innovations of later followers of Mohism.

The *History of the Han Dynasty*, "Monograph on Bibliography," records a *Mozi* in 71 sections; what have been transmitted to the present are only 53 sections; so 18 sections have been lost. The titles have been preserved of eight of these 18 lost sections: "Frugality in Expenditures," Part Two, "Frugal Burials," Part One, "Frugal Burials," Part Two, "Explaining Ghosts," Part One, "Explaining Ghosts," Part Three," "Against Music," Part Two, "Against Music," Part Three, and "Against the Confucians," Part One. According to the research of Sun Yirang, the remaining ten chapters have to do with expositions on weapons for defending against a siege, and methods of defensive warfare. Six of these sections are "Preparing Against Hooks," "Preparing Against Silting," "Preparing Against Smoke," "Preparing Against Tunneling," "Preparing Against Covered Carts" and "Preparing Against Wheeled Towers."

Hu Shi divided the 53 sections of the received version of the *Mozi* into five divisions:

First Division: "Befriending the Learned," "Self-Cultivation," "On Dyeing," "On the Necessity of Standards," "The Seven Causes of Worry," "Rejecting Excesses" and "Three Fold Argument," in all seven sections. ❶

Second Division: from "Elevating the Worthy," Part One to "Against Confucians," Part Two, in all 24 sections.

Third Division: "Canon," Part One and Two, "Canonical Explanations," Part One and Three, "Major Illustrations," "Minor Illustrations," in all six sections.

Fourth Division: "Geng Zhu," "Valuing Rightness," "Gongmeng," "Questions from Lu," and "Gongshu," in all five sections.

Fifth Division: from "Preparing City Gates" to "Miscellaneous Types of Defense," in all 11 sections.

This type of division has been accepted by the majority of scholars; however, doubts are held concerning the genuineness and date of composition of various sections, with each scholar maintaining a different viewpoint not

流传下来的墨家著作极少，最著名的是《墨子》一书。虽然这部著作题署著者为墨翟，但真正的作者其实并非墨子本人。中国先秦的古籍，尤其是诸子各书，大都是由门人弟子搜集整理师父的思想学说，逐渐编写而成的。成书过程往往要历经几代弟子，跨度甚至长达几百年时间。《墨子》便是墨子的弟子及其后学集体智慧的结晶。书中不仅注录了墨子的主要学说和思想，也包含了墨家后学的发展和创造。

《汉书·艺文志》著录《墨子》有七十一篇，流传至今的只有五十三篇，亡佚了十八篇。在这已经亡佚了的十八篇中，有八篇有存目：《节用下》、《节葬上》、《节葬中》、《明鬼上》、《明鬼下》、《非乐中》、《非乐下》、《非儒上》，其余十篇据孙诒让考证是关于守城器械和方法的论述，其中的六篇是《备钩》、《备冲》、《备堙》、《备空洞》、《备轒辒》和《备轩车》。

胡适将今本《墨子》的五十三篇分为五组❶，分别为：

第一组：《亲士》《修身》《所染》《法仪》《七患》《辞过》《三辩》，共七篇；

第二组：《尚贤上》——《非儒下》，共二十四篇；

第三组：《经上》《经下》《经说上》《经说下》《大取》《小取》，共六篇；

第四组：《耕柱》《贵义》《公孟》《鲁问》《公输》，共五篇；

第五组：《备城门》——《杂守》，共十一篇。

这一划分方法得到多数学者的认同，不过大家对各篇的真

---

❶ 胡适：《中国哲学史大纲》，上海古籍出版社，1997年，第108—109页。

❶ Hu Shi, *Outline of the History of Chinese Philosophy*, Shanghai Ancient Book Publishing House, 1997, pp. 108-109.

necessarily the same as the others.

Regarding the first division, Wang Zhong ever clearly indicated that the two sections of "Befriending the Learned" and "Self-Cultivation" were compiled by later followers who came after the original 70 disciples. Yet Hu Shi simply claimed that these seven sections were all fabrications by men of later times. Liang Qichao felt that the first three sections were not even the words of Mohists, and were all fake. However, he did not feel that the later four sections were later fabrications but were the records of later adherents summarizing Mohism, and had the function of indicating the main points of Mohist learning.

The main proof for claiming that the first division (especially the first three sections) was fabricated by later men was based on the following two points: (1) These sections contain many viewpoints similar to Confucianism; (2) They treat matters that happened after the death of Mozi.

Concerning the first point, many scholars have already refuted them. We know that Mozi once had "studied the learning of the Confucians, and received all of their knowledge." So before creating his own scholarly theories he had received a systematic education in Confucianism; therefore it is not strange that his early thought contains some Confucian flavoring. Moreover, such issues as "Befriending the Learned" and "Self-Cultivation" attracted much attention in the schools during the pre-Qin era; it is reasonable that Mozi would treat them in his own discourse. This point therefore cannot be used to refute the authority of Mohist authorship. As for the second point, that some events concerned historical matters that occurred after the death of Mozi, given the common precedent that all works of the philosophical masters were compiled after the death of these masters, the addition of some material after the death of Mozi is not proof that these sections were fabrications of others.

Concerning these points, we feel that the first division was formed by the editorial work of later followers of Mohism; it recorded the early thought of Mozi just after he had shrugged off the influence of Confucianism. "Although among these works were some theories close to Confucian thought, what was more important was that these theories already manifested the independent ideas of Mohists; even the first three sections were like this. For instance, the proposal for 'universal scholars' and 'universal lords' along the lines of the core theory of 'universal love,' advocated that 'the gentleman must debate,' clearly reflected a different attitude from that of Confucius. And the later four sections were even more closely related to such important theories as Mozi's 'Elevating the Worthy,' 'Will of Heaven,' 'Frugality in Expenditures' and

伪以及成书年代却各持已见，看法不尽相同。

关于第一组，汪中曾明确指出：《亲士》、《修身》二篇为七十子后学撰述。胡适则更为干脆地说这七篇都是后人假造的。梁启超也认为前三篇并非墨家之言，纯属伪托。不过他并不认为后四篇也是后人假造的，而是墨家后学记述的墨学概要，对理解墨学具有提纲挈领的作用。

认为第一组（尤其是前三篇）是后人伪造的主要根据有以下两点：（一）这些篇目中包含了许多与儒家近似的观点；（二）涉及了墨子身后之事。

关于第一点，已有许多学者进行过驳斥。我们知道，墨子曾"学儒者之业，受孔子之术"，在创立自己的学说之前曾接受过系统的儒家教育，因此他的早期思想带有些儒家味道并不足为怪。况且"亲士"、"修身"等问题先秦各家学派都十分关注，墨子有所论述也在情理之中，并不能就此否认墨家的著作权。至于第二点，即其中一些篇目涉及了墨子之后的历史事件，按诸子各书皆成于本人身后的通例，当是墨子后学整理时的添加，不能据此证明是他人伪作。

对此，我们认为，第一组由墨家后学编写而成，记录了墨子刚脱离儒家不久时的早期思想。"其中虽然有一些与儒家相近的理论，但更重要的是它们已经明确显示出墨家自己的主张，即使在前三篇中也是如此：比如涉及墨家核心理论'兼爱'的'兼士'、'兼君'的提出，主张的'君子必辩'也明显与孔子的态度不同。而后面四篇更是与墨子尚贤、天志、节用、非乐

'Against Music,' even to the extent of being able to regard them as outlines of these theories." ❶

The first 23 sections of the second division are called the "ten discourses" of Mohism; they contain the central thought of Mozi and the systematic theories of Mohism. Liang Qichao praised them as the grand outline of Mohist learning, and the nucleus of the book of *Mozi*. These 23 sections all contain the notation "Master Mozi said," demonstrating that none of them could have been written by Mozi himself but were formed at the hand of his disciples. There is no disagreement on this point in scholarly circles. As for the last section of this division "Against Confucians," because it runs contrary to Mohist thought, and because at the end of the section some language criticizing Confucius does not match with historical reality, it has always been suspected. Even though Mozi did not approve of many ideas of Confucius, he did not deny all Confucian ideas. According to the record of the section "Gongmeng," when Mozi and Chengzi were debating he once cited Confucius in a positive manner. Chengzi then asked Mozi why he both criticized Confucians and at the same cited Confucius. Mozi replied, "What is right is right and cannot be changed." It is evident that Mozi completely endorsed what was right in Confucius' thinking. Therefore Luan Tiaofu and other scholars feel that this particular section was probably composed during a period of fierce struggle between Mohists and Confucians by later followers of Mozi based on Mozi's thought in "Against Confucians," and was not a work transmitted down from Mozi himself.

This division also has a unique structure: each topic is divided into three sections—Part One, Part Two, and Part Three; their contents, structures and levels are also largely the same; yet the size gradually increases. As for this phenomenon, some scholars feel that Mozi divided his disciples into the three categories of doers, commentators and debaters; parts one, two, and three precisely fit into this grouping, and should be regarded as the result of these three types of disciples recording what they heard. Some scholars also feel that after "Mohism split into three schools," the disciples of these schools made different records. According to the way these three different parts cited the *Book of Poetry* and *Book of History*, as well as the difference of their dialects, Mr. Luan Tiaofu has tried to prove that part one of these "ten discourses" came from Qin period Mohists, part two came from Mohists in the east, and part three came from Mohists in the south.

Although each of these theories is reasonable, they also run counter to historical fact at some point. Each section in the "ten discourses" has simple language, is colloquial, and should be considered to be what disciples recorded

等重要理论密切有关，甚至可以视为其理论的纲要。" ❶

　　第二组前二十三篇被称作墨家"十论"，是墨子的中心思想，墨家的系统理论，梁启超称其为墨学的大纲目，《墨子》一书的中坚篇。这二十三篇中都有"子墨子曰"的字样，可知均不是墨子自著，而成于其弟子之手。这一点目前学界基本没有异议。至于这一组最后一篇的《非儒》，由于与墨子思想有违，且篇末指名批评孔子的一些文字与史实不合，历来被学者怀疑。墨子虽然不赞成孔子的许多思想，但他并非对儒家思想一概否认。据《公孟》篇记载，墨子与程子辩论时曾称述于孔子，程子问墨子为什么一边非儒一边又称述于孔子，墨子说："是亦当而不可易者也。"可见墨子对孔子思想中正确的部分也是十分赞同的。所以栾调甫等学者认为，这一篇大概是在儒墨两家抗争激烈之时，由墨家后学根据墨子"非儒"的思想自著而成的，并非述闻之作。

　　这一部分还有一个十分特别的结构：每一议题都有"上"、"中"、"下"三篇，其内容、结构和层次都大致相同，然而篇幅却在逐渐增长。对于这一特殊现象，有学者认为，墨子将自己的弟子分为从事、说书、谈辩三类，上、中、下正好与之相合，应该是这三类弟子各记所闻造成的结果。也有人认为它们是"墨离为三"后，三派弟子的不同记载。栾调甫先生还根据上、中、下三篇征引《诗》、《书》的多少以及方言的差别，考证出"十论"上篇出于秦之墨，中篇出于东方之墨，下篇出于南方之墨。

　　这些说法虽然各据其理，不过也都有不合事实之处。"十论"各篇文字质朴，语言多口语化，应该是弟子们在听墨子讲

❶ 秦彦士：《墨子与墨家学派》，山东文艺出版社，2004年，第22页。
❶ Qin Yanshi, *Mozi and the Mohist School*, Shandong Publishing House of Literature and Art, 2004, p. 22.

when they heard Mozi lecture. Therefore, records made at the same time should be largely similar, so how could they be augmented or reduced simply because of scholarly differences? What was rather more possible was that Mozi constantly lectured on the same topic over time; Part One was the record of his lectures during the initial period of him establishing the Mohist school; therefore it was rather short. Part Two was the record of his lectures made when Mozi was wandering around the various states ceaselessly developing his thinking, so it was comparatively fuller in content. Part Three was the adumbration of his mature thought late in his life, therefore it was the richest in content. Of course, we cannot deny that Mozi and his disciples as well as later followers edited these records. The "ten discourses" then were gradually formed by the unending improvement of Mozi, his disciples and later followers.

The six sections of the third division are collectively called the "Mohist Canon," and also called "Mohist Debate." They are rich in content, and treat philosophy, logic, psychology, political science, ethics, education, natural science and other areas; they may be termed an encyclopedia of the pre-Qin era. There are many different opinions concerning works in this division, and the matter has not been settled even today.

Those scholars represented by Hu Shi feel that none of these six sections were composed by Mozi himself, the reasons being the following four points: (1) The genre, grammar and diction are different from the various sections in the "ten discourses." (2) These six sections are all disquisitions by scientists and logicians, something the age of Mozi was incapable of composing. (3) In the section "Minor Illustrations," the title "Mohists" is used. (4) The issues discussed in these six sections are entirely the same as those fiercely debated during the time of Hui Shi and Gongsun Long; if these sections were not composed by those individuals, at least they were composed during their age.

Liang Qichao held to an opposing opinion. He felt that "Canon," Part One was without a doubt composed by Mozi himself. "Canon," Part Two was perhaps composed by Mozi or was a continuation by Qin Huali or Meng Sheng; I do not dare to decide the issue by conjecture.❶ He further point by point refuted Hu Shi's four reasons: (1) The various sections in the "ten discourses" of *Mozi* had been composed by Mozi's disciples; the fact that these six sections employed a different genre was precisely the proof that Mozi had himself composed them. (2) The explanations in the "Mohist Canon" on such concepts as "humaneness," "rightness," "employment," etc., were in line with Mohist's fundamental thinking. (3) The nature of each of these six sections was

授时的记录稿，因此同一时期的记录应当大致相同，怎么可能因为支派不同就随意增减呢？较为可能的是，墨子在不同时期常常就同一议题反复论述，上篇是他在建立墨家学派初期时的讲演记录，因此篇幅最短；中篇是游说诸国、思想不断发展时的讲演记录，因此较为丰满；下篇则是晚年思想成熟时的阐述，因此最为丰富。当然，我们不能否认墨子弟子及其后学对这些记录稿有所整理。"十论"是在墨子、墨子弟子和墨子后学的不断完善中逐渐形成的。

第三组六篇合称为《墨经》，也称作《墨辩》，包罗宏富，内容涉及哲学、逻辑学、心理学、政治学、伦理学、教育学、自然科学等诸多方面，堪称先秦时期的百科全书。关于这部分的作者，历来众说纷纭，至今仍无定论。

以胡适为代表的学者认为这六篇都不是墨子自著，理由有以下四点：（一）这六篇的文体、句法、字法都和"十论"诸篇不同；（二）这六篇全是科学家和名学家的议论，并非墨子时代所能作出；（三）《小取》篇中有"墨者"之称；（四）这六篇中讨论的问题全是惠施、公孙龙时代争论最激烈的问题，如果不是他们所作，也应该产生于他们那个时代。

梁启超对此持反对意见，他认为"《经上》必为墨子自著无疑。《经下》或墨子自著，或禽滑厘、孟胜诸贤补续，未敢悬断。"❶并对胡适提出的四条理由逐一进行驳斥：（一）《墨子》"十论"诸篇是墨子弟子所著，这六篇文体不同于它们，正是墨子自著的证明；（二）《墨经》中对"仁"、"义"、"任"等概念的解释与墨子的根本思想是一致的；（三）这六篇性质

---

❶ 梁启超：《墨经校释》，《饮冰室合集》第八卷专集之三十八，中华书局，1989年，第2页。

❶ Liang Qichao, *Corrections and Annotations on Mozi*, in *Collected Volumes from the Studio for Drinking Ice*, Vol. 8, Special Issue 38, Zhonghua Book Co., 1989, p. 2.

different from each other, so one cannot deny the composition of any section as deriving from Mozi just because any particular section had not been composed by him; (4) The issues discussed by Hui Shi and Gongsun Long constituted a small part of the "Mohist Canon," and the content was rather different. All that can be said of them was that the theories of Hui Shi and Gongsun Long found their origins in the "Mohist Canon," and cannot therefore presume that the "Mohist Canon" had been composed by them.

Still others feel that the six sections in the "Mohist Canon" were entirely the work of Mozi; at least the "Canon," Parts One and Three had been composed by Mozi. As for the real author of the "Mohist Canon," merely basing oneself on the extant historical materials would be difficult to reach a conclusion. At present what is rather more reliable is the theory of Yang Kuan: "The origin of the 'Mohist Canon' is the modern 'Canon,' Part One. The section 'Canon,' Part Two was written by some leader for use in a debate; his disciples used this as the basis of their debate, hence they also venerated it as a classic. In order to distinguish it from the original Mohist canon that was recited, they regarded the original Mohist canon as 'Canon,' Part One, and this later one as 'Canon,' Part Two." ❶ This means that the "Canon," Part One was composed by Mozi himself, and that the "Canon," Part Two was composed by later followers of the Mohist school. As for the two sections of the "Canonical Explanations," Parts One and Two, they were most likely composed by later followers of the Mohist shool to explain and annotate the language of the classic.

As for the five sections in the fourth division, there has been little divergent opinion over the ages. Hu Shi said, "These five sections were composed from materials gathered by later followers of Mohism based on the life and teachings of Mozi over the course of his life; this was similar to the *Analects*." ❷ Because in each section, of all of Mozi's disciples only Qin Huali is referred to as "Master Qinzi," we may conjecture that the author was one of the disciples of Qin Huazi. Because historical materials on Mohism have been rarely transmitted, these five sections have become precious resources for understanding the words and deeds of Mohists. There are even more original sources on Mohism than the "ten discourses," containing many early ideas from when Mozi first created this scholarly school. Add the various sections in the "ten discourses," and we can sketch out the main lines of argumentation of Mohist thought from when they were first created until they matured.

The eleven sections of the fifth division were works on military matters by the Mohists, and recorded the most famous of Mohism's defensive techniques.

各不相同，不能因其中某篇不是墨子自著就否认其他篇也不是墨子自著的；（四）惠施、公孙龙讨论的问题只是《墨经》中的一小部分，内容也颇为不同。只能说是惠施、公孙龙的学说源于《墨经》，而不能认为《墨经》是他们所作。

还有人认为《墨经》六篇全是墨子自著，至少《经上》、《经下》是墨子自己所作。至于《墨经》的作者究竟是谁，仅凭现有的史料很难作出定论。目前较为可信的是杨宽的说法："《墨经》原始，祇今经上篇；""经下一篇，当辩难时，某派之领袖所作，其徒以之为与辩者相辩之本者，故亦尊之为经，为别于原始原诵之墨经，乃以俱诵之墨经为经上，而以之为经下。"❶也就是说，《经上》为墨子自著，《经下》是墨家后学所作。至于《经说上》、《经说下》两篇，大概是墨家后学为了解释经文而后作的。

关于第四组的五篇，历来颇少异议。胡适说："这五篇，乃是墨家后人把墨子一生的言行辑聚来做的，就同儒家的《论语》一般。"❷因为各篇记述墨子弟子时只有禽滑厘被称作"子禽子"，我们由此推测作者就是禽滑厘的弟子。由于历史上流传下来的墨家资料极为罕见，这五篇成为我们了解墨家言行事迹的珍贵史料。这是比"十论"更为原始的墨家资料，包含了许多墨子刚刚创立墨家学派时的早期思想，再结合"十论"诸篇，我们便可勾勒出墨子思想从产生、发展到成熟的大致脉络。

第五组十一篇是墨家的军事著作，记述了墨家最负盛名的

❶ 参见杨俊光：《墨子新论》，江苏教育出版社，1992年，第44—45页。
❷ 胡适：《中国哲学史大纲》，上海古籍出版社，1997年，第109页。

❶ See Yang Junguang, *A New Discussion of Mozi*, Jiangsu Education Publishing House., 1992, pp. 44-45.
❷ Hu Shi, *Great Outline of the History of Chinese Philosophy*, Shanghai Ancient Book Publishing House, 1997, p. 109.

Because there are the high number of errors in the language of each section, and they treat many offensive and defensive weapons which have been long lost to history, these sections are therefore very hard to read. Most scholars regard this division as recording the defensive methods transmitted from Mozi to Qin Huazi, but some scholars suspect that it may be a forgery fabricated during the Han Dynasty. However, owing to the discovery of the Chu bamboo strips from Yunmeng, these suspicions are no longer tenable. Li Xueqin's article "Qin Strips and Each Section of the *Mozi* on Defensive Warfare" was based on the newly excavated Qin legal code; he demonstrated that the legal code, bureaucratic offices and penal system recorded in this division of the *Mozi* were all consistent with the legal code and bureaucratic titles of the Qin. Moreover, both systems share similarities in terms of such aspects as their systems of measurements and the format of the written characters. Therefore, Li Xueqin feels that these eleven sections "very possibly were the works of King Huiwen and Mohists of the later state of Qin." ❶

守御之术。由于各篇文字错落极多，而且涉及不少早已失传的
攻防器械，因此十分难读。学界一般都认为这部分是墨子传授
给禽滑厘的守城之法，但也有一些学者怀疑是汉代人的伪作。
不过随着云梦楚简的出土，他们的怀疑已不攻自破。李学勤先
生在《秦简与〈墨子〉城守各篇》一文中，根据出土秦律，论
证这一组记述的职官和刑法制度与秦在法律、职官名称方面具
有一致性，而且二者之间在计量制度、语词的书写格式等方面
也具有相似性。因此，李学勤认为这十一篇"很可能是惠文王
及其以后秦国墨者的著作"❶。

❶ 中华书局编辑部：《云梦秦简研究》，中华书局，1981 年，第324—335页。

❶ Zhonghua Book Co. Editorial Committee, *Investigation into Qin Strips from Yunmeng*, Zhonghua Book Co., 1981, pp. 324-335.

春秋晚期青铜器夫差盉
Bronze Drinking Vessel of King Fuchai of Wu
in the Late Spring and Autumn Period

五 探求真知，异彩纷呈

——《墨经》的主要成就

Chapter V Pursuing True Knowledge, Unusual Luster Exhibited in Profusion: The Major Accomplishments of the "Mohist Canon"

The "Mohist Canon" was also called "Mohist Debate;" it originally indicated the four sections of "Canon" Part One, "Canon" Part Two, "Canonical Explanations," Part One and "Canonical Explanations," Part Two in the book of *Mozi*. Lu Sheng of the Jin Dynasty wrote a book entitled *Annotations to Mohist Debate*. In his preface it said, " 'Mohist Debate' had a 'Canon' in parts one and two, with each part having an 'Explanation,' four sections in all." ❶ Sometimes Lu Sheng referred to this work as "Debating the Canon;" that is, researching and arguing over the "Canon." Afterwards, someone also included the two sections of "Major Illustrations" and "Minor Illustrations," and called all of these sections the "Mohist Canon." Because of its turgid and abstruse language, and the confusion in some of the order of the paragraphs and other errors that are rather numerous, the "Mohist Canon" has become one of the most difficult works to read in the whole of Chinese history. For the last two thousand years, it was very rare that any scholar bothered to annotate it. It was not until the end of the 19th century, following the spread of western learning into China, that Chinese intellectuals started to publicize democratic and scientific thought. They discovered that the "Mohist Canon" contained the scientific spirit and rational thinking that contemporary China completely lacked, and was able to enlighten the ignorant, liberate thinking, and was a powerful weapon to oppose feudal autocracy. Therefore, scholars started to annotate and investigate the "Mohist Canon," making the mysterious "Mohist Canon" gradually reveal its true countenance, like Mt. Lu in the famous poem of Su Shi.

The section "Canon," Part One in the "Mohist Canon" was not like other sections unified with a beginning and an end, and a core theme. Instead, its narrative was item by item, with each item explaining one definition, principle or concept; added to this was an annotation taken from "Canonical Explanations" explaining each item. The language of these two sections is extremely terse, strikingly different from the linguistic style of other sections. The layout of "Canon," Part Two is rather similar to "Canon," Part One. But at the end of each item was a note such as "the explanation is at such and such a place," or wording to the effect of "the reason being..." or "for instance," used to expound on the meaning of the previous exposition or to cite evidence. "Canonical Explanations," Part Two sometimes explained each item in the "Canon," Part Two, sometimes explained with examples what notes like "the explanation is found at such and such a place" indicated; the language was rather more detailed. "Canon," Part One contained approximately one hundred items, the format was rather in line with modern scientific definitions or

《墨经》也被称作《墨辩》，原本指《墨子》中的《经上》、《经下》、《经说上》、《经说下》四篇。晋朝人鲁胜有《墨辩注》一书，他在序中说："《墨辩》有上下《经》，《经》各有《说》，凡四篇。"❶鲁胜有时也称其为《辩经》，即研究辩论的"经"。后来又有人把《大取》、《小取》也算进去，一并称之为《墨经》。由于文字艰涩深奥，原文倒乱讹误处较多，《墨经》因此成为中国历史上最难读懂的著作之一，两千多年来罕有学者为之作注。直到19世纪末期，随着西学在中国的传播，中国的知识分子们开始宣扬民主和科学思想。他们发现，《墨经》中有着当时中国十分缺少的科学精神和理性思维，能够启发愚昧、解放思想，是反对封建专制的有力武器。于是学者们开始关注《墨经》、钻研《墨经》，使神秘的《墨经》逐渐露出了它的庐山真面目。

《墨经》中的《经上》篇不像《墨子》其他篇那样首尾贯一，有一个论说的中心主旨，而是分条而述，每一条都表述一个定义、原理或是概念，再由《经说上》对每一条加以解释说明。这两篇的文字都极为简约，和其他篇的语言风格迥然不同。《经下》体例略同《经上》，但每条最后都有"说在某某"的字样，也即"原因是"或"比如说"的意思，用以阐释前面的论说，或是举例论证。《经说下》或对《经下》各条进行阐释，或举例说明条目中"说在某某"所指为何，文字较《经说上》稍为详细。《经上》约一百条，其形式颇似今天各学科中的定

---

❶《晋书·隐逸传》。

❶ *History of the Jin Dynasty*, "Biographies of Recluses."

theories. "Canon," Part Two had about 80 items; some established Mohist arguments, some refuted the arguments of other schools.

This type of canon and commentary format exemplified by the "Mohist Canon" employed the format of analyzing a classic that was not a Mohist innovation in pre-Qin times. The Legalist work *Han Feizi* also employed the format of a "canon" section and its "explanation." However, these four sections of the "Mohist Canon" preserved an interesting feature: None of the items in the "Canon," Parts One and Two, correspond to the order of items in the "Explanation of the Canon;" instead they mix up odd and even, with every other one corresponding to the right item. This then is the "sideways" layout of the "Mohist Canon." This key to reading was discovered earliest by Bi Yuan. Based on the last note in the "Canon," Part One of "read this book sidewise," he deduced that the original format of "Canon" was one page divided into upper and lower parts. This means that the writing started with the upper part, first line on the right and worked towards the left, and then switched to the lower part and wrote from right to left. This writing layout saved silk, and means that all the upper lines were read first, then the lower lines. Afterwards, later readers erroneously read each line starting in the top part then continuing on through the lower part.

"Heading characters as title" was another unique formatting stylistic of the "Mohist Canon." It was first discovered by Cao Yaoxiang, and then codified by Liang Qichao as a general rule. It means that the first one or two characters of each item in the two sections of "Canonical Explanations," Parts One and Two, are the title characters of the canon, so it is very easy to identify the canon portion of the text. Based on the "reduplicated characters," we can also conveniently and quickly find the corresponding "explanation" portion of the text.

These two unique features of the format of the "Mohist Canon" were rarely seen in Chinese works over the course of history, and were the greatest hurdles to overcome by scholars researching the "Mohist Canon."

After clarifying the nature of these two great hurdles, scholars started to devote themselves to the content of the "Mohist Canon." They were astonished to discover that the "Mohist Canon," a short text of 10,000 words, contained such disciplines as philosophy, logic, psychology, political science, ethics, education and natural science; it can literally be considered to be an encyclopedia! According to statistics compiled by Hou Wailu's *Comprehensive History of Chinese Thought*, logic makes up the largest portion of the "Mohist Canon." Second is the content of natural science; third are ethics and morality;

义、定理之类。《经下》约八十条，有些则是建立自家论点，有些是批驳别家论点。

《墨经》这种有经有说、以说解经的形式在先秦并非独创，法家的《韩非子》中也有"经"与"说"的形式。不过《墨经》的这四篇却存在一个十分有趣的现象：《经上》、《经下》中各条与《经说》次序并不是一一对应，而是奇偶错综、隔条相对，这便是《墨经》独特的"旁行"体例。这种解读体例最早由毕沅发现。他根据《经上》最后的"读此书旁行"一语，推断《经》原本是分上下两栏排列，也就是说，写时先由上栏最右行起到最左行，然后再写下栏，由下栏最右行至最左行。这是一种节省绢帛的写法，应先读本绢帛的上行，再读下行。后来才被人们误作上下直行相连而读。

"牒字标题"是《墨经》的又一独特体例，由曹耀湘最先发现，梁启超后来将其定位公例。即：《经说上》与《经说下》两篇中每条的第一个字，或者前两个字，是这行经文的"标目字"，便于识别各条经文。根据"牒字"我们还可以方便快速地找到这条"经"的"说"文。

《墨经》这两种独特的体例为中国历代典籍所仅见，也就成为最初研究《墨经》的学者们的最大障碍。

在扫清这两大障碍之后，学者们开始致力于《墨经》内容的研究，他们惊讶地发现，短短不足一万字的《墨经》，却涵盖了哲学、逻辑学、心理学、政治学、伦理学、教育学、自然科学等多个学科内容，简直可以称得上是一部百科全书！据侯外庐《中国思想通史》第一卷统计，《墨经》讲逻辑学的最多，占第一位；其次是讲自然科学的内容；讲伦理道德的占第

fourth is psychology. Additionally, some economic theory and criticism of other philosophical schools are included.

When the topic of logic is mentioned, everyone first thinks of the founder of formal logic Aristotle. But very few people realize that at the same time that Aristotle was systematizing his logical studies, Mohists in China had achieved equally great results.

The study of logic in ancient China was called the study of names, debate, or study of names and debate; it flourished for a time during the Warring States Period when the hundred schools vied for attention. In order to verify their own theories in the midst of these "hundred schools vying for attention and to refute rival theories, each school highly emphasized debating skills, and actively researched the study of names as a tool of debate; this was especially true of the Mohists. In the course of this process, Mohists of the later school synthesized a set of special methods and principles.

The section "Minor Illustrations" said, "Debate can clearly differentiate the distinction between right and wrong, examine the sources to order chaos, distinguish clearly places that differ, observe the principles of name and substance, handle benefits and harm, and resolve suspicions." First of all, it explained from different angles the role of logic; afterwards it expressed the need to "broadly collect the phenomena and basic essence of all things, discuss and compare the differences in the various theories, use names to embody the various things, use words to express ideas, use language to explain and establish the reasoning behind one's words, and cite examples from similar categories to make judgments. This already clearly explained the logical method. Next it also mentioned that "What one has but others lack, cannot be censured; what one lacks but others have, cannot be sought from others." This points out the principles that should be adhered to when researching logic. It can be stated that the section "Minor Illustrations" was Mozi's concise outline of logic; it step by step defined the different forms and methods of reasoning. But the section "Major Illustrations" discusses many different issues in logic, systematically synthesizing and summarizing the process and conditions of reasoning. In addition to this, "Mohist Canon" also summarizes such methods of reasoning as supposition, selective speech, direct speech, deduction, induction, etc.; it announced such logical laws as the law of identity, the law of contradiction, and the law of the excluded middle, making Mohist logic become a system of systematic distinctions and order. This made it comparable to Aristotelian logical and ancient Indian hetuvidya logic as one of the three great schools of logic in the ancient world. Even though Mohist logic was

三位；讲心理学的占第四位；此外，还有一些经济政治理论和对别家学说的批判。

一提起逻辑学，大家首先想起的肯定是形式逻辑开创者亚里士多德，但很少有人知道，在亚里士多德对逻辑学进行系统研究的同时，中国的墨家学派在这一领域也取得了同样伟大的成就。

逻辑学在中国古代被称作名学、辩学或名辩之学，战国百家争鸣时期曾一度兴盛。为了在"争鸣"中证明己说、驳倒论敌，诸子各家都十分重视论辩技巧，积极研究作为论辩工具的名学，而以墨家尤甚。在这过程中，墨家后学们总结出了一套独具特色的名学体系。

对于论辩的功用、方法和原则，《小取》篇说："辩论可以明辨是非之分，审察治乱之因，辨明同异之处，观察名实之理，处理利害，决绝嫌疑"——首先从不同角度说明了逻辑学的作用；然后表示要"广泛搜求万物的现象和本质、讨论比较各种言说的异同、用名称来表达实物、用言辞来抒写意指、用语言来说明建立言辞的缘故、按照类别举例和做出论断"——这里已明确说明了逻辑学的方法。接下来又讲"自己有而他人没有的，不可非议他人；自己没有而他人有的，不可向他人求取"——则是提出了研究逻辑学应当遵循的原则。可以说，《小取》是墨家逻辑的简明纲要，它逐一定义了推理的不同形式和方法。而《大取》则讨论了众多的逻辑问题，系统总结和概括了推理的过程及条件。除此之外，《墨经》还总结了假言、选言、直言、演绎、归纳等多种推理方法，揭示了同一律、矛盾律、排中律等逻辑规律，使墨家逻辑成为一个系统分明、有条不紊的体系，与古希腊的亚里士多德逻辑和古印度的因明逻辑并称为世界三大古逻辑。虽然墨家逻辑在某些方面比之西方和印度的

different in certain respects from western or Indian logic, for instance lacking the formal system of the syllogism, and lacking a definite elaboration of inference, still its investigations into analogical inference greatly surpassed the relevant researches of western and Indian logic.

After the development of Mohist logic, it continuously influenced the mode of thinking of the Chinese, and elevated the level of thinking of the Chinese people, making a contribution that cannot be ignored. In this regard, the history of logic in China and the history of world logic both play important roles.

With regard to natural science, the accomplishments of the "Mohist Canon" are comparable to the science of ancient Greece. Its accomplishments in mathematics even reached the theoretical highpoint of the age. During the pre-Qin period of over two thousand years ago, the "Mohist Canon" provided scientific definitions for such geometric figures as the point, line, surface and body. For instance, "Canon," Part One said, "The extremity is the most random forward place of a body." The "Canonical Explanations," Part One said, "The extremity has nothing like it."

This means "body" is a part, and is opposite to "concurrent (the entirety)." It resides in the most forward extremity; the point which cannot be arranged is the "extremity." Because an "extremity" is in the front rank, and nothing in the front rank is comparable to it; therefore, the "Canonical Explanations," Part One said, "nothing is similar to it." The "extremity" mentioned here is equivalent to the "point" in European geometry, and is a fundamental concept of the geometry in the "Mohist Canon." The "Mohist Canon" contains a set of technical vocabulary from geometry: "extremity," "ruler," "region," "thickness;" these terms correspond respectively to the elements in geometric figures of the "point," "line," "surface," and "body."

The "Mohist Canon" also engaged in the scientific exposition of the relationships of distance, intersection and common tangents between the elements in geometric figures of the "point," "line," "surface" and "body." For instance, the "Canon," Part One said, "An interval means no thickness yet no contact." The "Canonical Explanations," Part One said, "An interval means no thickness yet there is some; this is possible."

In the same way, "contact" in geometry means "mutual intersection." Between two figures there is no space yet there is no mutual intersection ("an interval means no thickness yet no contact"), this is an "interval;" that is, it is the "common tangent" of geometry. "No thickness yet there is some; this is possible" then prescribed that the object is a figure that lacks volume.

逻辑学有所不同，例如没有设立三段论形式系统、没有关于推论式的明确论述，但它对类比推论的研究却大大超越了西方和印度逻辑的相关内容。

墨家逻辑产生之后就一直影响着中国人的思维方式，为提高中华民族的思维水平做出了不可忽略的贡献，这在中国逻辑史和世界逻辑史上均占有重要地位。

在自然科学方面，《墨经》的成就完全可以与古希腊的科学相媲美，其数学上的成就更是达到了彼时的理论高峰。在两千多年前的先秦时期，《墨经》就给点、线、面、体等几何图形作出了科学的定义，比如《经上》："端，体之无序而最前者也。"《经说上》："端，是无同也。"

在这里，"体"是部分，与"兼"（整体）相对，其中处于最前端、不参与排列的那一点就是"端"。因为"端"处于最前列，前面再没有与之相同者，所以"是无同也"。这里的"端"相当于欧几里得几何学中的"点"，是《墨经》几何学的一个基本概念。《墨经》中有一套几何学的专用词汇："端"、"尺"、"区"、"厚"，它分别对应几何图形的元素"点"、"线"、"面"、"体"。

《墨经》还对几何图形的元素"点"、"线"、"面"、"体"之间相离、相交、相切等关系进行了科学的阐述，如《经上》："次，无间而不相撄也。"《经说上》："次，无厚而厚，可。"

"撄"即几何学中的"相交"。两个图形之间既没有间隔也不相交（"无间而不相撄"）就是"次"，即几何学中的"相切"。"无厚而厚，可"则规定了讨论的对象不是有体积的图形。"厚"

"Thickness" explains a three-dimensional figure; "lacking thickness" indicates a line or surface with no thickness.

In addition to geometry, the "Mohist Canon" also investigated the problem of multiplication. "Multiplication means two." (The "Canon," Part One) "With two rulers and one ruler, merely get rid of one." (The "Canonical Explanations," Part One) Multiplication so-called means the number derived from taking an amount and multiplying it by two. For example, comparing two rulers with one ruler, from the number of two rulers remove one ruler and you will get one ruler.

With regard to physics, the "Mohist Canon" treated almost all branches of ancient physics. Like the Nobel Prize winner Ding Zhaozhong said when accepting his prize, "In the fourth century B.C., Mozi investigated the interaction between light and objects." [1] The "Mohist Canon" records experiments in optics, surprisingly similar to the results gained in recent experiments in optics. Mr. Qin Linzhao has said, "The earliest record in the world containing knowledge about optics is generally thought to have been by Euclid. His work contains language to the effect that light moves in a straight line... But it provides no evidence of any experimentation to verify this. What the 'Mohist Canon' records about the great discovery of the fundamental nature of light moving in a straight line has to be considered as being earlier than the record of Euclid, and is a better account." [2] Assuredly, the part in the "Mohist Canon" concerning optics was already quite complete; it systematically elaborated on such fundamental issues in optics as the definition of shadows and its genesis, the principle of the rectilinear propagation of light, projecting images through pinholes, the principle of the reflection of light as well as the spherical mirror, projecting images through lens, etc.

The "Mohist Canon" recorded for the first time in the history of Chinese science an optical experiment on projecting images through pinholes. "As for the scene, the man in the light warms like an arrow, the person below grows tall, and the tall person grows short. The foot is covered by light, hence it forms a scene above; the head is covered by light, hence it forms a scene below. Both near and far scenes have extremities together with the light, hence the scene is stored within." [3]

In this passage, "warmth" is an error for "to shine" and "man" is an error for "to enter." "Extremity" is a pinhole, and "together with" means "to interfere;" "the scene being stored within" means a screen to be used to form an image. The meaning of this sentence is that a line of light shines into a small pinhole then, just like shooting an arrow, the light shot out from below passes

说的是立体图形，"无厚"是指没有厚度的线或面。

除了几何学，《墨经》还研究了倍数的问题："倍，为二也。"（《经上》）"二尺与尺，但去一。"（《经说上》）所谓倍数，就是把该数乘以二所得之数。比如二尺与一尺相比，从二尺中减去一尺就得到一尺。

在物理学方面，《墨经》几乎涉及了古物理学的所有分支。诺贝尔物理学奖得主丁肇中在领奖时说："墨子在公元前四世纪就曾研究光和物质的相互作用。"[1]《墨经》中关于光学实验的记录，与近代光学实验的结果惊人的相合。钱临照先生曾说："世界光学知识最早的记录，一般的说法是属于欧几里得的。在他那书里有一段记录光是直线进行的文字。……但找不出用任何实验来证明。……光是直线进行的基本性质的伟大发现，《墨经》所说的要比欧几里得来得早，并且来得好。"[2]的确，《墨经》中关于光学的部分已形成相当完整，它系统地论述了物影的定义和成因、光的直线传播原理和小孔成像原理、光的反射原理以及球面镜、透镜的成像规律等光学的基本问题。

《墨经》中记载了中国科学史上第一次小孔成像的光学实验："景，光之人煦若射，下者之人也高，高者之人也下。足蔽下光，故成景于上；首蔽上光，故成景于下。在远近有端与于光，故景库内也。"[3]

在这里，"煦"为"照"之误，"人"为"入"之误，"端"即小孔，"与"为"干预"之意，"景库"是指用来成像的影屏。这句话的意思是说，光线照入小孔就像射箭一样，从下面射来

---

[1] 参见王讚源：《中国第一奇书〈墨经〉》，《职大学报》2002年第3期。
[2] 参见任继愈：《墨子与墨家》，商务印书馆，1998年，第122页。
[3] 《经说下》。

[1] See Wang Zanyuan, "The First Extraordinary Book in China, the 'Mohist Canon,'" *Journal of Vocational University*, 2002, Issue 3.
[2] See Ren Jiyu, *Mozi and Mohism*, The Commercial Press, 1998, p. 122.
[3] "Canonical Explanations," Part Two.

through the pinhole towards a higher point, and the light shot down from above penetrates the pinhole towards a lower point. The foot blocks the lower light, therefore it forms an image above; the head blocks the light from above, so it forms an image down below. Whether far off or nearby, a small pinhole interferes with the movement of the light, therefore it forms a reverse image on the other side.

In addition to recording this experiment in optics, the "Mohist Canon" also produced some marvelous theoretical summaries regarding some phenomena concerning mechanics. For instance, in the "Canon," Part One, "force is the means by which a form moves." (Force is the reason that a physical entity moves or transforms). This is the remarkably similar to Newton's second law.

Archimedes once boasted: "Give me a fulcrum, and I could move the world." The English scholar Joseph Needham discovered after his researches that Mohists had already grasped what Archimedes had said about the theory of complete equilibrium. The "Canon," Part Two records, "If it is integral and not mixed, then it will correspond." (If a balanced pole maintains its state of equilibrium, it is because the weight from either end is equivalent). The word "to correspond" thoroughly describes the condition of motion of a balanced pole given a state not at equilibrium. Even though he did not accurately express the lever principle in a formula, from the context we can see that Mohists had already grasped the essence of the principle of the lever. They furthermore utilized it in the process of engineering for production, for life, and for military equipment, designing and manufacturing the well-sweep, the pulley block and other types of simple machines.

In addition to this, the "Mohist Canon" also set relatively firm definitions and expositions concerning such empty concepts as space and time. For instance, "duration refers to differences in time;" "space, means different places." ❶ "Duration" is what we would today call time and "space" indicates the modern concept of space. The meaning of these two sentences is, "Time encompasses different periods of time; space encompasses different types of locations." This is astonishingly similar to the content of Aristotle's concept of "location." The "Mohist Canon" also took an additional step in investigating the characteristics of time and space, pointing out that both time and space are limitless, and that the march of time is able to induce changes in space.

With regard to ethics and morality, society and politics, the "Mohist Canon" inherited and expounded on Mozi's theory of universal love, bringing

的光线通过小孔到达高处，从上面射来的光线通过小孔到达下方。脚挡住了下面的光线，所以成像于上方；头挡住了上面的光线，所以成像于下方。在远处或近处有小孔干预了光线的行进，所以光线在另一边形成了倒像。

除了记录光学实验，《墨经》还对自然界的一些力学现象作出了精妙的理论概括。比如《经上》中"力，形之所以奋也。"（力是物体运动变化的原因。）这与牛顿第二定律何其相似！

阿基米德曾自豪地说："假如给我一个支点，我可以撬起地球。"英国学者李约瑟研究后发现，墨家已经掌握了如阿基米德所说的全部平衡理论。《经下》记载："贞而不挠，说在胜。"（衡木保持平衡状态，是因为两端所加重量相等。）对应《说》文详细描述了衡木在各种不平衡状态下的运动情况，虽然并没有以精确的公式表达杠杆原理，但从中可以看出墨者已经掌握了杠杆原理的精髓。他们还将其运用于生产、生活和军事工程中，设计和制造出了桔槔、滑车等简单机械。

除此之外，《墨经》还对空虚无义的时空观念进行了相当深刻的界定和阐述。如："久，弥异时也"、"宇，弥异所也"❶。"久"是今天所说的时间，而"宇"指的就是空间。这两句话的意思是说，"时间，涵盖各种不同的时段。空间，涵盖各种不同的处所。"这与亚里士多德的"处所"这一空间概念的内涵也有惊人的相似之处。《墨经》还进一步研究了时间和空间的特性，指出时间与空间都具有无限性，时间的推移能够引起空间的变化。

在伦理道德和社会政治方面，《墨经》继承和发扬了墨子

---

❶《经上》。

❶ "Canon," Part One.

up the proposition that "humaneness is group love." ❶ "Group love," so-called, is loving others just as one loves oneself. This type of love which treats others no different than treating oneself is the only kind of love that can be called "humaneness." This type of definition can be regarded as a summation of Mozi's theory of universal love. As for "rightness," the "Canon," Part One, records the definition that "rightness is benefit," regarding "rightness" as being completely equal to "benefit." It took a further step and regarded "benefit" as the core, and set definitions for such moral characteristics in ethics as "loyalty" and "filial piety," and promoted Mozi's utilitarianism to a new degree.

Even though all the philosophical schools flourished in the same pre-Qin period, why was Mohism the only school to establish a new school, leaving behind the "Mohist Canon," rich in scientific thinking and argumentation? In his *The Origins of Mohism*, Fang Shouchu gave voice to one of the main reasons: "Mozi basically emphasized knowledge, and together with his disciples, participated in many practical production industries. After a long time of accumulation, he gained rich personal experience; later followers continued in this same spirit and organized it, explained it, and so the accomplishments of this school were unique and lofty. At the time, there were other important schools, such as Confucianism, which sought knowledge was largely in the realm of chanting and explaining; Taoists, who largely emphasized profound thinking; Logicians, who largely played games with language and writing, and so all of them divorced themselves from production relationships." ❷

Mr. Liang Qichao said that the Mohist Canon was a pearl of great price bequeathed to us by our forefathers. It not only is a priceless jewel in Chinese intellectual history, it is also a scintillating star in the history of the development of world scientific technology and logic.

的兼爱学说，提出"仁，体爱也"❶的著名命题。所谓"体爱"，就是像爱自己那样的爱别人，这种对待他人和自己没有差别的爱才可以称之为"仁"。这样的定义可以看作是对墨子兼爱学说的总概括。关于"义"，《经上》中定义为"义，利也"，将"义"与"利"完全等同，并进而以"利"为核心，为"忠"、"孝"等伦理道德做出定义，将墨子的实利主义推上了新的高度。

　　同处于先秦时期，为什么诸子百家中只有墨家独树一帜，留下了《墨经》这样富有科学思辨特点的著作呢？方授楚在《墨学源流》中道出了其中的主要原因："墨子本注重知识，又与其弟子，多参加实际生产事业。日积月累，亲身之经历既多，后学继此精神加以组织之，说明之，故成绩独为高卓也。当时重要学派，如儒家之求知识，多在诵说，道家多重冥想，名家则颇以文字语言为游戏，因均脱离生产关系也。"❷

　　梁启超先生说《墨经》是祖宗遗下的无价之宝。它不仅是中国学术史上的无价之宝，也是世界科学技术和逻辑学发展史中的璀璨之星！

❶《经上》。
❷ 方授楚：《墨学源流》，中华书局、上海书店出版社，1989年，第177页。

❶ "Canon," Part One.
❷ Fang Shouchu, *The Origins of Mohism*, Zhonghua Book Co., and Shanghai Bookstore Publishing House, 1989, p. 177.

六 俭节则昌，淫佚则亡

——墨家的经济思想

Chapter VI　Frugality Leads to Flourishing, Indulgence
Leads to Destruction: Mohist Economic
Thought

As the spokesman for the common class, Mozi very much stressed the economic life of the state and the masses of the people. Economizing and valuing frugality were his fundamental economic thinking. Targeting the extravagant and luxurious life of the ruling class, Mozi sounded the alarm for the ruling class of "frugality leads to flourishing, indulgence leads to destruction," ❶ and strove to promote the thought of "frugality in expenditures" and "frugality in burials."

Frugality in expenditures, so-called, was to cut down on expenditures, opposing all "unnecessary costs." Mozi hoped that the rulers would be able to accomplish "supply to the people all that is necessary for their use, but stop when it increases costs without increasing benefits". ❷ This means that consumption is fine as long as it maintains a basic living standard, but do not engage in consumption that cannot increase benefits to the people. If all rulers were able to be so "frugal in expenditures," then the state could save a great amount of expenses, and the wealth of the state would double. In such aspects as clothing, food, dwellings, travel and burial, Mozi proposed to cut down on expenses to a reasonable degree.

As for clothing, Mozi proposed the principle that they should "be able to withstand the cold in the winter, and be able to withstand the heat in the summer." ❸ In the winter black clothing should be worn that was both light and warm; in the summer coarse burlap should be worn which was both light and cool. Mozi felt that if clothing could accomplish this, then it was enough, and there was no need to seek excessive luxury. As for "casting gold into hooks, and using pearl and jade as ornament," ❹ it was too luxurious and should be stopped since it "increased costs without increasing the benefits to the people."

As for food and drink, Mozi was completely opposite to Confucius' "eat nothing but the finest, and nothing but the daintiest." ❺ Instead, Mozi proposed to allay hunger and revitalize the energy, to strengthen the limbs and make the eyes and ears work well, and that was good enough; there was no need to excessively worry over spices and flavors and no reason to seek rare and precious foods from distant states.

As for dwellings, Mozi felt that all that was necessary was to withstand the damp, wind, rain and snow, and to have walls to separate men from

作为平民阶级的代言人，墨子非常重视国家和民众的经济生活，节约尚俭是他最基本的经济思想。针对当时统治阶级奢侈靡乐的生活，墨子为他们敲响"俭节则昌，淫佚则亡"❶的警钟，并大力倡导"节用"、"节葬"思想。

所谓节用，就是节约开支，反对一切"无用之费"。墨子希望统治者能做到"凡足以奉给民用诸，加费不加民利则止"❷。意思是说，消费只要能维持基本生活条件就可以了，不再进行不能为人民增添利益的消费。如果统治者都能这样"节用"，那么国家便可省去大量费用，国家的财富将增加一倍。在衣、食、住、行、葬等各个方面，墨子都提出了节用所应把握的合理分寸。

对于衣服，墨子提出"冬以圉寒、夏以圉暑"❸的原则。冬天穿深青色的衣服，又轻便又暖和；夏天穿粗麻布的衣服，又轻便又凉爽。墨子认为，穿衣做到这样就足够了，没必要过分追求奢华。至于"铸金以为钩，珠玉以为佩"❹的做法，过于奢侈，"加费不加于民利"，应该废止。

对于饮食，与孔子的"食不厌精，脍不厌细"❺相反，墨子倡导饮食只要能够充饥补气，强壮四肢，使人耳目聪明就可以了，不需要过分讲究调料和味道，更没必要追求远方国家珍贵稀罕的食品。

对于住房，墨子认为房屋只要可以抵御潮湿风寒和雪霜雨

❶《辞过》。
❷《节用中》。
❸《节用上》。
❹《辞过》。
❺《论语·乡党》。

❶ "Rejecting Excesses."
❷ "Frugality in Expenditures," Part Two.
❸ "Frugality in Expenditures," Part One.
❹ "Rejecting Excesses."
❺ *Analects*, "Xiangdang."

women. There was no need to waste human labor or materials to build sumptuous and luxurious dwellings.

As for means of transportation, Mozi felt that in the manufacture of boats and chariots, as long as they "were sturdy and light" and could "accommodate heavy loads and travel far", then that was all that was required. The purpose of riding chariots or taking boats was entirely for the sake of ease of transportation; therefore, such practices as "adorning chariots with decorations and colors, and adorning boats with ornate carvings" ❶ were all extravagant expenditures.

Starting out from the viewpoint of being frugal in expenditures and targeting such contemporary social practices as "lavish burials," Mozi proposed the theory of "Frugal Burials" and opposed the harm to society brought on by burials and funerals. Confucians had all along advocated "luxurious burials and long-term mourning." Confucius' disciple Zai Wo once was berated by Confucius as not being humane for pointing out that "three years of mourning was too long a period." ❷ Concerning this, what Mozi advocated was completely opposite. He criticized the contemporary social practices of insisting that coffins be multi-layered, that burials be luxurious, that the burial vestments of the deceased be in several sets, and that the graves be large and stately, as inhumane and unrighteous practices, and he illustrated the various kinds of dangers brought about by "luxurious burials and long-term mourning."

First of all was the huge expense involved. After the death of a king, nobleman or other aristocrat, the living must exhaust all of the valuables and money in their storehouses, decorating the deceased with gold, jade and jewels, and bind them up with sashes knit from silk and cotton; furthermore, horses and chariots must serve as grave goods to be placed in the grave. Also, the following items must be placed by the side of the corpse: curtains, drums, low tables and mats, mirrors, dagger-axes, swords, plume banners, ivory tusks, leather skins and the like; sometimes even the living were buried alive to accompany the dead. Doubtless, these practices were a great waste of the wealth created by the people, and could only cause the state and the people to grow more and more impoverished.

Next, after a lavish burial, a long period of mourning was necessary, which not only wasted social productivity but also harmed the increase of population. For during the three year period of mourning, the nobility could not concern themselves with political affairs, peasants could not plow fields, craftsmen could not engage in production, and women could not weave and

露，砌墙壁使男女分开住就可以了，没必要耗费人力与物力将房屋建造得富丽堂皇。

对于交通工具，墨子认为制造舟车只要能"完固轻利"，"任重致远"就行了。乘车、船的目的完全在于交通的方便，因此"饰车以文采，饰舟以刻镂"❶之类的做法都是奢侈浪费。

墨子从节用的观点出发，针对当时社会"厚葬久丧"的做法提出"节葬"之说，反对为丧葬而贻误社会生产。儒家一贯主张"厚葬久丧"，孔子的学生宰我曾因提出"三年之丧，期已久矣"而被孔子斥为"不仁"❷。对此，墨子的主张完全相反，他批评当时社会流行的棺木一定要有多层、埋葬必须深厚、死者衣服必须多件、坟墓必须高大的做法是不仁不义的行为，并列举了厚葬久丧的种种危害。

首先是对财物的巨大浪费。在王公贵族去世后，活着的人必须倾尽府库贮藏的所有财宝，将金玉珠宝装饰在死者身上，用丝絮织带束住，并把车马随藏在墓穴中。还要将帷幕、鼓、几筵、镜子、戈、剑、羽旄、象牙、皮革等物品一并埋在死者身旁，甚至还要用人殉葬。这样的做法无疑是将民众创造的财富大量浪费，只会使国家和人民越来越贫穷。

其次，厚葬之后还要长时间服丧，既荒废社会生产，也不利于人口增殖。在三年之丧期间，王公贵族无法过问政事，农夫不能在田地耕作，百工不能从事生产，妇女无法纺纱织布。

---

❶《辞过》。
❷《论语·阳货》。

❶ "Rejecting Excesses."
❷ *Analects*, "Yanghuo."

knit. In addition to this, long periods of mourning would "ruin men and women relations," ❶ influencing the increase of population. This would result in "a state that would inevitably become poor, a population that would inevitably become sparse, and an administration that would inevitably be chaotic;" this would provide the opportunity and condition for other states to invade. Mozi concluded from this that lavish burials and long periods of mourning result in everything harmful but nothing beneficial, and he insisted that they be abolished.

Well then, how could one actually be frugal in burials? Mozi advocated that coffins could only be three inches thick, which was enough for the remains of the deceased to decay inside and that would be good enough. All that was necessary was three pieces of vestments, enough to block the noxious smells of the decaying corpse from leaking out, and that would be good enough. As far as how deep the coffin should be, as long as the bottom does not touch the springs and the top does not leak out noxious smells, a grave three feet wide would be enough. Since the deceased is already peacefully interred, the living has no need to cry and grieve, but should hurry and resume engaging in production; this would be beneficial to both the living and the dead.

Another embodiment of "frugal expenditures" was "Against Music." Mozi advocated being frugal in cultural and entertainment aspects. He felt that Confucian "Ruining the whole world" included "strings and song, drums and dancing in the form of vocal music." ❷ Rulers held concerts and dances on a large scale, doubtlessly exploited the wealth of the broad mass of the people in the form of food and clothing, something that must be opposed. Mozi felt that the mass of the people suffered from three great hardships: "The hungry cannot find food, the cold cannot find clothing, and the laborers cannot find rest." ❸ Yet when the ruling class hold one large scale music concert and dance performance, they will use thousands of performers in the performance. If these performers do not eat and dress well, their facial expressions would not be beautiful and alluring, their voices would not be moving to auditors, their movements would not be graceful. Therefore, they need to eat fine food, wear beautiful costumes, but these all depend on the hard work of a large mass of laborers to be provided. If the people once become enamored of music, then nothing would get done. The nobles and aristocracy would not hold early court audiences or retire late from court, or adjudicate legal cases because of being enamored of music. Scholars and gentlemen would not spend their energy in managing the government, the reception of tax revenues, or fill up the warehouses and government storehouses because of

除此之外，久丧还会"败男女之交"❶，影响到人口的增殖。这样的结果只会是"国家必贫，人民必寡，行政必乱"，为别国的侵犯提供机会和条件。墨子由此认为，厚葬久丧百害而无一利，必须坚决废止。

那么，究竟该如何节葬呢？墨子主张：棺木只要三寸厚，足以使死者的尸骸腐烂在里面就够了；衣服只要三件，足以阻挡尸体腐烂的臭气外溢就可以了。至于下葬，只要下面不掘到泉水，上面不漏出臭气，坟墓有三尺宽就可以了。死者既已安葬，活着的人也没必要长时间的哭泣哀伤，而应该赶紧从事生产，这才是对生者和死者都有利的事。

"节用"的另一体现是"非乐"。墨子主张在文化娱乐方面也要节约，他认为儒家"足以丧天下"的另一件事就是"弦歌鼓舞，习为声乐"❷。统治者们大办音乐歌舞，这无疑是在剥夺广大民众的衣食之财，必须加以反对。墨子认为，民众有三大忧患："饥者不得食，寒者不得衣，劳者不得息"❸。而统治者举办一次大型音乐歌舞，就要成千上万个演员来参加。这些演员如果吃穿不好，脸色就会不美艳，声音就会不动人，动作就会不优雅。所以他们要吃精美的食物，穿漂亮的衣服，而这些都要靠广大劳动者的辛勤劳动来提供。人们一旦迷恋上了音乐，就什么事也不能做了：王公贵族因为迷恋音乐而不早上朝、晚退朝、不听审案件；士人君子因为迷恋音乐而不花费精力去治理官府、征收赋税、充实仓廪府库；农夫因为迷恋音乐而不早出晚归地耕田、植树、种菜；妇女因为迷恋音乐而不起

---

❶《节葬下》。
❷《公孟》。
❸《非乐上》。

❶ "Frugal Burials," Part Two.
❷ "Gongmeng."
❸ "Against Music," Part One.

being enamored of music. Peasants would not get up early and stay late to till the fields, plant trees or sow vegetables because of being enamored of music. Women would not work from early till late weaving silk, flax and cotton because of being enamored of music. Actually, it was not that Mozi did not realize the beauty of music. Mr. Wu Feibai said, "Mozi being against music did not mean that he did not appreciate music; it was merely a measure to save the world in an emergency." ❶ During the pre-Qin period when the material production of society was not developed, Mozi had to give up spiritual wealth, and first seek material benefits.

While advocating thrift, Mozi also promoted a new emphasis on production. Mozi pointed out that production was the essential difference between man and beast. In human society, "those who rely on their own strength survive; those who do not rely on their own strength do not survive." ❷ Those who rely on their own power are able to survive; if not, then they will perish. This is to say that in the language of today that "those who do not work do not eat." Starting out from this point, Mozi stressed that every person had to engage in production, and opposed those who gained anything without working for it. Only through each person striving to labor would the wealth of the world be sufficient, and would society be able to develop in stability, and the people be able to live and work in peace and happiness. Therefore, Mozi appealed to the people to actively engage in production and to strive to accomplish things. He further admonished the peasants to increase the time they devoted to laboring, to elevate the intensity of labor, advocated practicing early marriage to increase the population of laborers, and personally set an example of the ideological thinking of encouraging agriculture and being moderate in expenditures. He claimed for himself that he "ate according to the measurement of his belly, and wore clothing according to the size of his body;" what his disciples wore were "short coarse coats" and what they ate were "coarse stews." ❸ Under these conditions of hard working and plain living, they were industrious in production, creating a large number of implements of military application and for the use of the people. Their industry reached the extent of being so tired that the flesh dropped from their calves, and their shins were rubbed clear of leg hair.

Sima Tan's "Treatment of the Essentials of the Six Schools" mentioned that "Mozi's encouragement of agriculture and being moderate in expenditures" was something that could never be lost. In the present age of the 21st century, this sentence still possesses a strong element of practical significance.

早贪黑地纺纱、绩麻、织布。其实墨子并不是不知道音乐之美，伍非百先生说："墨者非乐，非不知乐。为救世之急也。"❶在社会物质生产尚不发达的先秦时期，墨子不得不舍弃精神财富，而先追求物质之利了。

主张节约的同时，墨子还提倡重视生产。墨子指出，生产是人与动物相区别的本质特征。在人类社会，"赖其力者生，不赖其力者不生"❷，依靠自己力量的人才能生存，反之则不能生存，也就是今天所说的"不劳动者不得食"。从这一观点出发，墨子强调人人都要从事生产，反对不劳而获。只有每个人都努力劳动，天下的财富才会充足，社会才能稳定发展，人民才可能安居乐业。因此，墨子号召人们积极生产，勉力而为。他还规劝农民增加劳动时间、提高劳动强度，主张实行早婚的风俗以增加劳动人口，并身体力行其强本节用的思想学说。他自称"量腹而食，度身而衣"，他的弟子穿的是"短褐之衣"，吃的是"藜藿之羹"❸。就在这样艰苦朴素的条件下，他们辛勤生产，制造了大量军用和民用器械，以至于累得腿肚子上都没有了肉，小腿上也磨去了汗毛。

司马谈《论六家之要旨》中说墨子"强本节用，不可废也"。在21世纪的今天，这句话依然具有很强的现实意义。

---

❶ 参见杨俊光：《墨子新论》，江苏教育出版社，1992年，第136页。
❷《非乐上》。
❸《鲁问》。

---

❶ See Yang Junguang, *A New Interpretation of Mozi*, Jiangsu Education Publishing House, 1992, p. 136.
❷ "Against Music," Part One.
❸ "Questions from Lu."

春秋晚期青铜器纹饰
Decorations on the Bronze Vessel
in the Late Spring and Autumn Period

七 兼相爱，交相利

——墨家的伦理思想

Chapter VII　Embracing Universal Love, Engaging in What is Mutually Beneficial: The Ethical Thinking of Mohism

Mozi's ethical thinking revolved around expounding on the fundamental thesis of embracing universal love and engaging in what is mutually beneficial. The *Spring and Autumn Annals of Mr. Lü* says, "Mo Di valued what was embraced by all." The basic meaning of "to embrace" was one hand holding two stalks of rice; the extended meaning was to concurrently tend to several aspects of the same matter. In the "Mohist Canon," "embracing" indicated "the entirety," or "all" of something. Therefore, what universal love in the main stressed was the breadth of the scope of love, it required one to "universally love all persons in the world." ❶ In Mozi's view, whether it was oneself or others, whether one's background was noble or base, every man was the target of love; the scope of the target of this love should be "the people in the world," or the entirety of humanity. This is to say that "the great breadth of universally loving all the world, is comparable to the universal brilliance of the sun and moon shining on the world without partiality." ❷

Why is universal love necessary? Mozi felt that the reasons society of the time was in such tumult and the feudal princes engaged in wanton military action were both because of the lack of mutual love between men: the feudal princes only know how to care for their own states, so do not care about other states; therefore they would raise the entire power of the state to attack other states. Families only know how to care for their own clans, so do not know how to care for other clans; therefore they raise the entire power of their clan to plunder other clans. People only know how to care for their own lives, and do not care for the lives of others; therefore they do their best to slaughter other people. The feudal princes do not love each other, so war between states is inevitable; heads of families do not love each other, so clans plunder each other. Men do not love each other, so this inevitably leads to slaughter among men. Lords and ministers do not love each other, so this inevitably leads to no love or loyalty among them.Fathers and sons do not love each other, so inevitably there is no kindness or filial piety. Brothers do not love each other, so inevitably there is no closeness or cooperation. If all the people in the world do not love each other, well, the strong will inevitably control the weak, the rich will inevitably insult the poor, and noble persons will inevitably disdain base persons, the deceitful persons will deceive the simple persons. Therefore, all calamities, plundering and blood feuds in the world are produced by the lack of mutual love. Targeting these types of social realities he prescribed the right medicine. The effective medicine he prescribed to save the world was "universal love." As long as states, families and men were all able to practice

墨子的伦理思想是围绕着"兼相爱、交相利"这一基本论点展开的。《吕氏春秋》说："墨翟贵兼"。"兼"的本义是一只手拿着两棵稻谷，引申为同时顾及事物的几个方面。在《墨经》中，"兼"表示"整体"、"全部"的意思。因此，兼爱主要强调的是爱的范围的广泛，要"兼爱天下之人"❶。在墨子看来，不管是自己还是别人、无论出身是高贵还是低贱，只要是人，都是被爱的对象，这个爱的对象范围应该是"天下之人"，也就是整个人类，也即"兼爱天下之博大也，譬之日月兼照天下之无有私也"❷。

为什么要兼爱？墨子认为，当时的社会之所以混乱动荡、诸侯之所以穷兵黩武，都是因为人与人之间的不相爱：诸侯只知道关爱自己的国家，却不关爱别人的国家，所以才会举全国之力去攻打别的国家；家主只知道关爱自己的家族，却不关爱别人的家族，所以才会举全家之力去掠夺别的家族；人们只知道关爱自己的生命，却不关爱别人的生命，所以才会使出浑身解数去残杀他人。诸侯之间不相爱，就必然发生国与国的战争；家主之间不相爱，就必然会有族与族之间的掠夺；人与人之间不相爱，就必然导致人与人之间的残杀；君臣之间不相爱，就必然没有恩惠和忠心；父子之间不相爱，就必然没有慈爱与孝顺；兄弟之间不相爱，就必然没有和睦与协调。如果全天下的人都不相爱，那么，强者必然控制弱者，富者必然欺侮贫者，显贵的人必然傲视低贱的人，奸诈的人必然欺骗憨厚的人。所以，凡天下的祸患、掠夺与怨恨，都是由人们之间不相爱而产生的。针对这样的社会现实，墨子对症下药，他开出的救世良

---

❶《天志下》。
❷《兼爱下》。

❶ "Will of Heaven," Part Two.
❷ "Universal Love," Part Two.

"embracing universal love," all of this confusion and lack of coordination would no longer exist.

Mozi's "universal love" especially stressed that love could not distinguish between close and distant relatives or noble and base statuses— all should be loved the same; this was different than the thinking of "humane love" taught by Confucius. Confucians advocated "graded love," that is, to dispense different degrees of love based on the closeness or distance of relationships. Starting from protecting the constant relationships of "lord to lord, minister to minister, father to father, and son to son," ❶ Confucius advocated starting from one's individual position in the course of dispensing love, then gradually expanding outward towards others. Therefore, with the distances of proximity and farness, the differences of important and insignificance, during this course of dispensing love, the more distant a relationship was, the less love was manifested. The "Geng Zhu" records a debate between Mozi and the Confucian follower Wumazi; this prominently demonstrated the feature of "graded love" of the Confucians. Wumazi said to Mozi, "I love the people of the state of Zou more than I love the people of the state of Yue, but I love the people of Lu more than the people of Zou, and love the people of my homeland more than I love the people of Lu. I also love my family members more than I love the people of my homeland, and love my parents more than I love my family members, and love myself more than I love my parents. This is all because I am closest to myself." The love of Confucians was founded on blood-ties, and proceeded from the inside out; from "loving the closest" it gradually extended to "loving the people" and "loving the masses;" what was protected and strengthened was naturally the patriarchal clan system. Yet Mozi smashed through the barrier of the blood-ties based on the patriarchal clan system, and strove to oppose the "differentiated love" of Confucians with their "techniques of cherishing relatives and the gradations of venerating the worthy." ❷ This type of love was certain to incite "great harm in the world;" therefore Mozi clearly proposed the idea of "universality replacing gradation." ❸

In order to implement the thought of "Universal Love," Mozi equated it with the will of "Heaven." He also demanded that the people regard "Heaven" as the highest object to emulate. This was quite similar to Christianity's "charity." The Bible regarded human nature as fraught with weakness, therefore men must follow Heaven as their standard. In addition, the "charity"

方就是"兼爱"。只要国与国、家与家、人与人之间都能做到"兼相爱"，这一切混乱与不协调都将不复存在。

墨子的"兼爱"特别强调爱要不分亲疏、不分贵贱，对一切人一律同等爱之，这与孔子的"仁爱"思想有所不同。儒家主张"爱有差等"，即根据亲疏贵贱而施予不同程度的爱。从维护"君君，臣臣；父父，子子"❶的纲常出发，孔子主张在施行爱的过程中以自己为起点，逐渐扩大至他人。因此就有了近与远的距离，有了厚与薄的差异，在这过程中，关系越远表明爱的程度就越低。《耕柱》中记载了墨子与儒家之徒巫马子的一次辩论，就突出表现了儒家这种"差等之爱"的特点。巫马子对墨子说："我爱邹国人胜于爱越国人，爱鲁国人胜于爱邹国人，爱我家乡的人胜于爱鲁国人，爱我的家人胜于爱家乡的人，爱我的父母胜于爱我的家人，爱我自己胜于爱我的父母。这都是因为更切近自身的缘故。"儒家的爱以血缘关系为基础，由内向外，由"爱亲"产生渐而推及"爱民"、"爱众"，所维护和强化的依然是封建的宗法制度。而墨子则冲破了宗法血缘的藩篱，极力反对儒家这种"亲亲有术，尊贤有等"❷的"别爱"，认为这样的爱必将引起"天下之大害"，从而明确提出"兼以易别"❸的主张。

为了推行"兼爱"思想，墨子把"兼爱"作为"天"的意志，并要求人们以"天"为最高的取法对象，这与基督教的"博爱"颇为类似。《圣经》认为，人性中有许多缺点，所以人

❶《论语·颜渊》。
❷《非儒下》。
❸《兼爱下》。

❶ *Analects*, "Yan Yuan."
❷ "Against the Confucians," Part Two.
❸ "Universal Love," Part Two.

of Christians also advocated loving others as oneself, and loving all men equally.

With regard to the issue of "Universal Love," Mozi recognized the difference in gradations between people, but still demanded that all love each other equally with no distinctions. This unavoidably led to the trap of internal inconsistency. Actually, in a class society, this type of supra-class "Universal Love" was merely a kind of beautiful phantasy; it had no social foundation for being realized. Because of the limitations of history, Mozi was unable to comprehend the emptiness of the thought of universal love. In order to strengthen the possibility of implementing universal love in practical life, he proposed the law of causality of "throw me a peach, and I will return to you a plum;" just so, those who love others will necessarily be loved by others; those who benefit others will necessarily be benefited by them. But those who detest others will necessarily be detested by others; those who harm others will necessarily be harmed by others. As long as one bases himself on this principle in his treatment of others, others will certainly base themselves on the principle of love to requite him. Loving others is the premise and condition for others to love oneself. If all of the people in the world were able to love others, then oneself would naturally be include within the scope of those being loved. Therefore, "Universal Love" included others, and included oneself; that is, "loving others does not exclude the self, the self is included in this love." ❶ Yet Christianity likewise regards people as having a reciprocal type of nature. *The Book of Mathew* writes, "In any circumstance, do unto others as you would have them do unto you, because this is the law and the prophets." It is just that the love of Christ goes one step further than "Universal Love" in requiring that people requite injury with virtue, and those whom should be loved include one's enemies and the evil, just as Jesus said, "I say unto you, do not contend with the evil. If someone strikes you on the right cheek, then turn the left cheek for him to strike; if someone tells you that he wants to take your coat, then let him take your cloak as well."

Tightly connected with "Embracing Universal Love" was Mozi's utilitarian moral principle of "Engaging in What is Mutually Beneficial." Mozi constantly mentioned "Embracing Universal Love" in conjunction with "Engaging in What is Mutually Beneficial." According to his viewpoint, love

必须以天为准则。除此之外，基督教的"博爱"也主张爱人如爱己，平等地爱一切人。

在"兼爱"的问题上，墨子认同人与人之间存在着等级差别，却又要求人们不分差别地彼此相爱，这就不可避免地陷入了自相矛盾的泥潭之中。其实，在阶级社会中，这种超阶级的"兼爱"只能是一种美好的幻想，根本没有实现的社会基础。由于历史的局限，墨子不可能意识到兼爱思想的空想性。为了增强兼爱在现实生活中运行的可能性，他提出了"投我以桃，报之以李"的爱的因果律原则:关爱别人的人，别人也必定关爱他；给别人利益的人，别人也必定给他利益；憎恶别人的人，别人也必定憎恶他；残害别人的人，别人也必定残害他。只要自己本着爱的原则去对待他人，别人也一定会本着爱的原则来回报自己，爱他人是他人爱自己的前提和条件。如果天下所有人都能爱别人，那么自己自然也包含在被别人爱的范围之中，因此，"兼爱"既包含了别人，也包含了自己，也就是"爱人不外己，己在所爱之中。"❶而基督教同样认为人有一种相互回报的本性，《圣经·马太福音》中写到："无论何事，你们愿意人怎样待你们，你们也要怎样待人。因为这就是律法和先知的道理。"只不过基督之爱比"兼爱"更进一步要求人们以德报怨，所爱之人甚至包括仇敌和恶人，就像耶稣所说："只是我告诉你们:不要与恶人作对。有人打你的右脸，连左脸也转过来由他打；有人想要告诉你，要拿你的内衣，连外衣也由他拿去。"

与"兼相爱"紧密相联的，是墨子"交相利"的实利主义道德原则。墨子经常把"兼相爱、交相利"并提，在他看来，

---

❶《大取》。

❶ "Major Illustrations."

meant benefit, and benefit meant love. "Embracing Universal Love" was an internal moral sentiment, and "Engaging in What is Mutually Beneficial" is concrete action expressing this kind of moral sentiment. Without an actual "benefit" there is no need to mention "love."

Confucianism "rarely mentioned benefits." Confucian felt that, "The gentleman is informed by rightness, the petty man is informed by benefits." ❶ Yet Mozi not only valued rightness but also emphasized benefits, and insisted on a unified view of rightness and benefits. At this point, what Mozi meant by benefits was not private benefits but the benefits of the people. To Mozi, rightness was the need to "stimulate the benefits in the world, and eliminate the harm in the world;" only actions that let the people gain concrete benefits is able to be considered right actions. Mozi felt that "the sage has love but no benefits" was a precept of the Confucians, and was a theory of outsiders; but Mohists advocated both "love" and "profit" being mentioned together, regarding such viewpoints of humaneness, rightness and love as directly linked with benefits and utility. Therefore, while promoting "embracing universal love," Mozi further demanded that the people "engage in what is mutually beneficial." As long as each person "engaged in what is mutually beneficial," it would be possible to ultimately achieve the social ideal of "embracing universal love."

Mozi not only promoted universal love, but also he led his disciples to do their utmost to bring about universal love. He took achieving peace in the world as his personal mission, and wandered to the four corners of the world to save the world, to the extent of "his calves had no fuzz, his shins had no hair." ❷ In order to achieve the social ideal of universal love, his disciples even went so far as to "walk in fire and tread on knives, and would not retreat in the face of death." ❸

Mozi's thinking on universal love, especially the glorious record of Mohist achievement in concrete actions, not only set lofty moral examples for the Chinese people, but also demonstrated the great spiritual strength of humanity. Today, given globalization and modernization, and in the face of increasing individualism and egotism, promoting Mozi's ideal of universal love and seeking to achieve the path toward this idealism still possess extremely important practical significance. It is exactly as the famous historian Arnold J. Toynbee said, "Mozi's theory of regarding universal love as a moral obligation is even more appropriate to advocate for the modern world, because

爱就是利，利即为爱。"兼相爱"是内在的道德情操，而"交相利"则是由这种道德情操外发出来的实际行为。没有实际的"利"，就无从谈"爱"。

儒家是"罕言利"的，孔子认为："君子喻于义，小人喻于利" ❶。而墨子却既贵义又重利，坚持义利统一的观点。在这里，墨子之利，并非一己之私利，而是人民之利。在墨子看来，所谓的义就是要"兴天下之利，除天下之害"，只有能让人民得到切实利益的行为才能算作义举。墨子认为："圣人有爱而无利"是儒家的言论，是外人的说法，而墨家则主张"爱利"并言，即把仁、义、爱等观念同利益、功利直接联系起来。因此，在提出"兼相爱"的同时，墨子还要求人们做到"交相利"。只有人人都做到了"交相利"，才能最终实现"兼相爱"的社会理想。

墨子不仅提倡兼爱，而且带领弟子不遗余力地去实践兼爱。他以天下太平为己任，为救世而四处奔走，以致"腓无胈，胫无毛" ❷。他的弟子为了实现兼爱的社会理想，甚至都可以"赴火蹈刃，死不还踵"。❸

墨子的兼爱思想，尤其是墨家光辉的实践行为不仅为中华民族树立了崇高的道德典范，而且也显示了人类伟大的精神力量。在全球化和现代化的今天，面对日益盛行的个人主义和利己主义，倡扬墨子的兼爱理想，寻求实现这一理想的道路，依然具有十分重要的现实意义。正如著名历史学家汤因比所说："把普遍的爱作为义务的墨子学说，对现代世界来说，更是恰

---

❶《论语·里仁》。
❷《庄子·天下》。
❸《淮南子·泰族》。

❶ *Analects*, "Liren."
❷ *Zhuangzi*, "The World."
❸ *Huainanzi*, "Taizu."

the modern world is already unified in terms of technology. But with regard to feelings, we still have not become unified. Universal love is the only hope in the world of saving ourselves. Mozi's love is even more needed by modern people than Confucius' love." ❶

当的主张，因为现代世界在技术上已经统一，但在感情方面还
没有统一起来。只有普遍的爱，才是人类拯救自己的惟一希望。
墨子的爱比孔子的爱更为现代人所需要。" ❶

❶ 参见孙君恒：《墨子的经济伦理与市场经济模式》，《武汉科技大学学报》（社会科学版）
2000年3月第2卷第1期。

❶ See Sun Junheng, "Mozi's Economic Ethics and the Model of a Market Economy," *Journal of the Wuhan Technical University*, 2000, Vol. 2, Issue 1.

墨子善于城守攻防的研究

Mozi Being Good at the Research of Defending
against Sieges and the Offensive or Defensive

八　非攻救守，积极防御

——墨家的军事思想

Chapter Ⅷ　Against Offensive Warfare and Saving through
Defensive Warfare, Aggressive Defense:
Mohist Military Thought

"Universal Love" was the core of Mohist ethical thinking. Mozi felt that the reason for the appearance in society of such phenomena as the strong seizing the weak, the majority plundering the minority, the wealthy insulting the poor, and the noble lording it over the base lay in the lack of mutual love between individuals. From this point of departure Mozi developed an important content of his military thought—against offensive warfare. Universal love was the foundation of his ethics, and the anti-warfare thought was an extension of universal love.

The age in which Mozi lived was a transitional period from a slave society toward a feudal society. Therefore it was the age in Chinese history most frequently beset by war. Struggles between states, usurpation among household, wars large and small were too many to even count: In 447 B.C. the state of Chu destroyed the state of Cai; in 423 B.C. the state of Han attacked the state of Zheng; in 414 B.C. the state of Yue destroyed the state of Teng; in 412 B.C. the state of Qi invaded the state of Lu... Society was in turmoil in the midst of such fierce warfare; the people became destitute and homeless, and had no means of livelihood. Mozi intensely realized the great calamities brought on to the people by warfare, so he raised the great banner of "Opposing Offensive Warfare" without hesitation, strongly denouncing unrighteous wars.

His opposition to offensive warfare was an opposition against the mutual pillaging between the various feudal states and the clans within the states and instead advocated peaceful settlement of difficulties. Mozi called all the prevalent plundering and warfare of the Spring and Autumn and Warring States Periods unrighteous wars. He cited as an example the case of a man going to another man's orchard to steal peaches and plums; if word got out he would be despised, if government officials found out he would be punished because stealing the property of others was "harming others to benefit the self;" it was unrighteous behavior that damaged others to benefit the self. If the stealing took place in other men's households to plunder cattle or horses, it would be even less righteous than stealing peaches and plums because it would cause others to suffer even greater losses. Following this line of thinking, Mozi continued extrapolating and said that when a great state pillaged a minor state, plundering the land and people of the other state, would not that be even more unrighteous than stealing cattle and horses? Nowadays, the gentry and gentlemen in the world all know that stealing other person's peaches and plums, cattle and horses is unrighteous conduct, yet they regard the pillaging that occurs in offensive warfare as an immortal achievement; they all know

　　"兼爱"是墨子伦理思想的核心，墨子认为社会上之所以出现强执弱、众劫寡、富侮贫、贵傲贱的现象，根源就是人与人之间的不相爱，由此出发，引发出墨子军事思想的重要内容——非攻。兼爱是非攻的理论基础，非攻是兼爱的延伸。

　　墨子生活的时代，是由奴隶社会向封建社会过渡的时期，因而也是中国历史上战争最为频繁的时期。国与国相争，家与家相篡，大大小小的战争不计其数：公元前447年楚国灭亡蔡国，公元前423年韩国攻打郑国，公元前414年越国灭亡滕国，公元前412年齐国侵略鲁国……社会在激烈的征战中动荡不安，人民流离失所，民不聊生。墨子真切体会到战争给人民带来的巨大灾难，毫不犹豫地举起"非攻"大旗，强烈谴责非正义的战争。

　　所谓非攻，就是反对诸侯国之间、国内各家族之间的互相掠夺攻伐，倡导和平相处。墨子将春秋战国之际盛行的掠夺兼并战争称为不义之举。他举例说，如果有人到别人的果园里去偷取桃李，人们听说后就会鄙视他，官府知道后就会惩罚他，因为偷窃别人的东西就是"亏人自利"，是损人利己的不义行为；如果到别人家中偷取牛马，是比偷窃桃李更为不义的行径，因为这样会使他人受到更大的损失。顺着这条思路墨子继续推理说：大国侵略小国，掠夺别国的土地和人民，那不是比偷窃牛马更为不义的行为吗？现如今，天下的士人和君子都知道偷窃别人的桃李、牛马是不义之举，却将攻伐掠夺之战当作不朽的功业；都知道杀一个人是有罪的，而战争中死伤的人又何止

that killing a man was a crime, yet how are the dead in a war limited to a thousand or ten thousand yet people insist on praising these casualties as the result of a righteous endeavor? "Stealing a dog or a pig is called inhumane; stealing a state or a city is taken to be righteous." ❶ This really is something hard to figure out!

After morally evaluating offensive warfare as unrighteous behavior, Mozi furthermore concretely analyzed the danger and harm brought about by warfare:

First, warfare interferes with labor and production, and wears out the people and squanders resources. Mozi said, "Fighting during spring causes the fields to lie fallow and prevents plowing and sowing; fighting during the fall hinders the harvest and storage of crops by the people. Such a delay wastes an entire season, and the common people will suffer from hunger and cold, and starve or freeze to death in incalculable numbers." Rulers engage in wanton military activities and frequently start wars, the short ones lasting for several months and long ones lasting for several years. But with the common people involved in long-term campaigning, they cannot sow or harvest on schedule. If things continue in this way, the foodstuffs of the state will certainly be insufficient, and the people inevitably will endure hunger and cold.

Second, warfare diminishes the population, creating a shortage in the labor pool. Mozi said, "Even if one attacks a small walled state of six or seven *li* square, it will still cause the death of several thousands of men, perhaps upwards of ten thousand men. If one attacks an even larger state, the casualties will be even more serious. Now the land of many large states remains uncultivated, lacking the labor force to open up this land. Rulers do not devise means to increase population, but instead pay the price of sacrificing a large number of troops to occupy the territory of other states." Acting in this way is certainly "abandoning more of what you lack, and emphasizing that which you have in abundance." ❷

Third, warfare not only reduces population, it also wastes a great amount of the wealth of a society. Warfare wastes armor, shields, spears, halberds, etc., and the wastage of the food and fodder, cattle and horses, and chariots that are necessary for warfare is also a huge amount. But the booty gained from warfare sometimes is not as much as was spent on the warfare, therefore to say that a war was conducted to pillage and plunder is a gain not equal to the loss.

Fourth, regardless of whether the people are from the victorious state or from the losing state, the people will suffer greatly from warfare. In each battle the greatest victims will be the common people; even the people from

千万，可是人们却偏偏将其称为义举。"窃一犬一彘则谓之不仁，窃一国一都则以为义" ❶，这真是让人无法理喻的事啊！

在从道德评价上将攻伐之战定义为不义之举后，墨子又具体分析了战争所带来的危害：

第一，战争会耽误劳动生产，劳民伤财。墨子说："春天打仗会荒废百姓翻耕种植；秋天打仗会耽误百姓收获聚藏。这样荒废了一季，百姓因饥寒而饿死、冻死的不计其数。"统治者穷兵黩武，频繁起战，时间少则数月，多则数年。而百姓长期出征在外，无法按时播种收获。长此以往，国家的粮食储备必然不足，百姓挨饿受冻就不可避免。

第二，战争使人口减少，造成劳动力短缺。墨子说："即使攻打一个方圆六七里的小城，也得死伤数千乃至上万人。如果要攻打更大的国家，那么死伤一定会更加惨重。现在许多大国土地荒芜，缺少劳动力进行开垦。统治者不想办法增加人口，反而以牺牲大量士卒为代价去侵占别国的土地。"这样的做法实在是"弃所不足，而重所有余也" ❷。

第三，战争不但造成人口减少，而且会浪费大量的社会财富。战争会造成甲、盾、矛、戟等兵器的损耗，战争所需的粮草、牛马和车辆的消耗也是一个巨大的数字。而战后获得的战利品有时还没有自己消耗的财富多，所以说进行以掠夺为目的的战争是得不偿失的。

第四，无论对战胜国的人民还是对战败国的人民，战争都会给他们带来深重的灾难。每一次战争，受苦难最深的都是老

---

❶《鲁问》。
❷《非攻中》。

❶ "Questions from Lu."
❷ "Against Offensive Warfare," Part Two.

the victorious side will be displaced and die in a foreign land or suffer the pain of losing relatives. The people from the losing side will suffer even a worse calamity; their property will be confiscated, their lives perhaps exterminated, and many people will perhaps be enslaved.

Therefore, Mozi stood on the side of the laboring people and severely denounced the strategy of wars of aggression; "if repeated wars of aggression occur, this would be the greatest harm in the world." ❶

Mozi's opposition to offensive warfare did not mean that he opposed all warfare; he felt that wars could be divided into wars of offense and wars of punishment; that is, there are divisions of righteous and non-righteous wars. As for such cases as Yu campaigning against Youmiao tribe, Tang attacking Jie, and King Wu sending a force out against Zhou, Mozi expressed no opposition. What he opposed was only wars of aggression when the large attacked the small, or the strong seized the weak. In the face of aggression, Mozi advocated an aggressive defense on the part of the aggrieved party, the complete mobilization of the people, and a vigorous opposition instead of waiting passively for death. Mozi not only voiced his criticism against acts of aggression, but he led his disciples to personally help protect and defend besieged cities in states that were being invaded; from this experience he synthesized a systematic theory of defensive warfare. At the time, such sayings as "the defense of Mo Di" and "Mozi was skilled at defense" gained currency. Sima Qian once critically evaluated Mozi as being "skilled at defensive warfare," and so up to the present time people still mention the notion of "a Mohist defense."

Mozi's defensive thinking is concentrated in each section of the *Mozi* related to defending against siege warfare. We already know that the language in these 11 relevant sections was written by later followers of Mozi, but was the method of defending against sieges taught by Mozi to Qin Huali; it reflects in a concentrated manner his defensive thinking and the techniques for defending a city.

Combat readiness was an important issue that involved the survival or death of a state. Mozi completely emphasized combat readiness. He said, "Being prepared is the important task of the state." ❷ He stressed on multiple occasions the importance of "preparing foodstuffs," "preparing weapons" and "preparing walled cities": "Food is the treasure of the state; weapons are the claws of the state; walled cities are how we defend ourselves. These three are all tools of the state." ❸ In addition to this, Mozi further stressed "preparation in plans;" that is, one must prepare for effectively engaging in

百姓，即使是战胜国的人民也会遭受背井离乡、客死他乡或者丧失亲人的痛苦；战败国的人民更是灾难深重，他们财产被掠夺，生命被杀戮，还有许多人沦为奴隶。

所以，墨子站在劳动人民的立场上强烈谴责侵略战争，"当若繁为攻伐，此实天下之巨害也"❶。

墨子讲非攻，并不是说反对一切战争，他认为战争有"攻"与"诛"，即有正义与非正义之分。对于像禹征有苗、汤伐桀、武王伐纣之类的正义战争，墨子并没有任何的反对。他所反对的只是以大攻小、以强执弱的侵略战争。在面临侵略时，墨子主张被侵略国积极防御、全民动员、奋起反抗决不束手待毙。墨子不仅在口头上谴责侵略行径，而且带领弟子亲自参与被侵略国的守城保卫战，并从中总结出积极防御战的系统理论。在当时就有"墨翟之守"、"墨子善守"的术语流行，司马迁曾评价墨子"善守御"，直到今天人们还有"墨守"一说。

墨子的防御思想集中体现在《墨子》一书城守各篇之中。我们已经知道，这十一篇文字都为墨家后学之作，是墨子传授给禽滑厘的守城之法，集中反映了墨子的防御思想和守城之术。

战备是关系到国家存亡的重大问题。墨子十分重视战备，他说："备者，国之重也。"❷他一再强调"备粮"、"备兵"、"备城"的重要性："食者，国之宝也；兵者，国之爪也；城者，所以自守也。此三者，国之具也。"❸此外，墨子还特别强调"备虑"，即在思想上也要做好战争的准备，"心无备虑，不可

❶《非攻下》。
❷《七患》。
❸《七患》。

❶ "Against Offensive Warfare," Part Three.
❷ "Seven Disasters."
❸ "Seven Disasters."

war in the matter of theory. "If the mind is not prepared with plans, then one cannot respond to the unexpected misfortunes." ❶ Mozi further felt that small states should unite together, and defend in common against the aggressive actions of large states. "If a large state attacks, then unite to save it." ❷ During a long period of practical experience, Mozi gradually synthesized a set of effective defensive tactics. First of all was to "enlist the entire population as troops." In the face of a strong enemy and weakness at home, and given the situation of a numerous army of enemies and few troops on our side, it was necessary to mobilize all possible forces to engage in defense. Mozi also organized all officers into a top-down hierarchy, counting from the bottom with such divisions as the rank-and-file soldiers, a squad leader in charge of five, a sergeant in charge of ten, a centurion, a major, a general, a commander and a prefectural commander; it was tightly organized and orderly. He made a rational organization of each unit. Next, Mozi especially stressed the need to be strict and fair in rewards and punishments, for "rewards should be clear and dependable and punishments should be strict and fear-inducing." ❸ Those with merit should be generously rewarded, and those who do not obey orders should be severely punished, even to the extent of being beheaded. Only in this way will every order be executed without fail and troops will be effectively led. As for the deployment of troops, Mozi made the following arrangements: On city walls, each step should have five armored troops with halbreds; every five steps should have a five-unit squad leader; every ten steps should have a sergeant in charge of ten troops; every hundred steps should have a centurion. Each side of a walled city should have a commanding officer, and the overall commander should be in the middle of the city. In order to preserve ease of communications on the battle field, he utilized beacon fires, sundials, banners, drums and oral orders to set up a complete system of communication. Mozi further created ten or more defensive weapons: arrow barriers, straw carts, moat sheds, siege towers, shadoofs, long axes, long awls, long hoes, iron hasps, turrets, suspended objects and repellers. In addition to this, with regard to defensive engineering, Mozi also had many independent views. First was the need to strengthen and increase the height of city walls and to deepen moats. Second was the need to erect two-tiered gates or sluice gates in city walls, to encase wooden city gates in copper or iron. Third was to erect on city walls facilities for making observations to help in keeping the enemy under surveillance.

Mozi's opposition to offensive warfare and practical activities fighting against aggression was supported and praised by the large mass of people; it

以应卒"❶。墨子还认为弱小的国家应该联合起来，共同抵制大国的侵略行为，"大国之攻小国也，则同救之"❷。在长期战争实践中，墨子逐渐总结出一套行之有效的防御策略：首先是"举全城之民皆兵"，面对敌强我弱、敌众我寡的形势，必须动员一切可以动员的力量投入到防守中去。墨子还将部队的隶属关系自上而下分为士卒、伍长、什长、佰长、尉、将、帅、郡守等不同等级，严密有序，将部队合理地组织起来。其次，墨子特别强调要赏罚严明，"赏明可信而罚严足畏"❸。对有功者要重赏，而对于不服从命令者，就要严惩直至处斩，只有这样才能令行禁止，有效地指挥军队。在兵力部署上，墨子是这样安排的：城墙上，每一步有带甲持戟士兵五人，每五步有一名伍长，十步有什长、百步有佰长。城的每一面有一名指挥官，城中为主将所在地。为了确保战场通讯顺畅，他利用烽火、树表、举旗、击鼓、口传等建立起完整的通讯系统。墨子还创制了十多种守城器械：渠谵、藉车、行栈、行楼、颉皋、长斧、长椎、长兹、距、飞冲、批屈等。此外，在防御工程的修建方面，墨子也有许多独到的见解：一是要加固加高城墙、挖深壕沟；二是城门要设门、闸两层，木制城门的外面包以铜铁；三是在城墙上设立观察设施，便于监视敌人。

墨子的非攻主张和反对侵略的实践活动得到了广大人民的

---

❶《七患》。
❷《非攻下》。
❸《备城门》。

---

❶ "Seven Disasters."
❷ "Against Offensive Warfare," Part Two.
❸ "Preparing Walls and Gates."

retains an important guiding significance even today for preserving world peace. Each section in *Mozi*, "Siege Defense," and *The Art of War* that advocated the techniques of offensive warfare, have been praised as the "twin jewels in the Chinese history of ancient military history." ❶

拥护和赞扬，至今仍对维护世界和平具有重要的指导意义。
《墨子》的"城守"各篇与鼓吹进攻之术的《孙子兵法》，也被
称作中国"古代军事学史上的双璧"。❶

❶ 孙中原：《墨学通论》，辽宁教育出版社，1993年，第306页。

❶ Sun Zhongyuan, *General Introduction to Mohism*, Liaoning Education Publishing House, 1993, p. 306.

九 尊天事鬼，神道设教

——墨家的宗教学说

Chapter IX Venerate Heaven and Serve Ghosts, Setting up Religion to Teach the Way of the Spirits: Religious Doctrines of Mohism

　　Reverence for Heaven above and superstitious belief in ghosts were primitive beliefs held in common by the ancestors of all nationalities of the world, and the Chinese nationality was no exception. During the Shang period, this type of primitive religious belief was rather prevalent, and the people attributed every marvelous happening that was hard to explain as being due either to the will of Heaven or to the actions of ghosts and spirits. Following the advance of society and civilization and the elevation of the level of human knowledge, belief in the Heavenly Ancestor and ghosts and spirits had started to waver within the human heart by the Zhou Dynasty. Confucius did not mention the matter of ghosts and spirits; "the master did not mention strange happenings, feats of strength, rebellion or spirits." ❶ Confucius even said, "If one does not know about life, how can one know about death?" ❷ This means that when we cannot grasp the meaning of all aspects of human life, how will we be able to grasp matters concerning life after death? However, Mozi who was born after Confucius, indulged in unbridled propaganda when he proclaimed the existence of Heaven above and ghosts and spirits, and did his utmost to play up their supernatural powers.

　　Mozi felt that the will of Heaven above was the most supreme, and even the Son of Heaven must submit to this heavenly will. He cited the following example: If the Son of Heaven got sick, then he would prepare sacrificial offerings to Heaven and to the ghosts and spirits in prayer. Afterwards, Heaven above would eradicate his illness. However, it has never been heard that Heaven above prayed to the Son of Heaven; therefore, he said that Heaven is more venerable than the Son of Heaven. Not only did Mozi feel that Heaven had a will, but also did his utmost to verify that ghosts and spirits also existed. He first cited passages in the *Book of Xia*, the *Book of Shang* and the *Book of Zhou* that were relevant to ghosts and spirits. Following this, he further cited a whole series of examples: King Xuan of Zhou killed Du Bo in error, and three years afterwards, the spirit of Du Bo killed King Xuan with an arrow to take revenge; Duke Mu of Qin was a man of humaneness and morality, therefore the spirit personage Goumang materialized in broad daylight, reporting that Heaven above had extended his life for 19 more years; Duke Jian of Yan killed the innocent Zhuang Ziyi, and later on the spirit of Zhuang Ziyi appeared to take revenge, killing Duke Jian in his chariot; During the era of Lord Wen of Song, a priest was not obeying the rules for making sacrificial offerings, and as a result he was killed by the spirits on the altar; Two great ministers of the state of Qi Wang Liguo and Zhongli Jiao were fighting in a law suit, they let a sheep that was possessed by a spirit be the judge, and the result was that Zhongli Jiao

对上天的敬畏和对鬼神的迷信是世界各族先祖共同有过的原始信仰，中华民族亦不例外。在殷商时期，这种原始的宗教信仰是相当普遍的，人们把世界上各种难以解释的奇妙现象大都归结为上天的意志或鬼神的作用。随着社会文明的进步和人类认识水平的提高，到了周代，天帝、鬼神的信仰在开始在人们心中动摇。孔子对于鬼神之事就闭口不提，"子不语怪、力、乱、神" ❶。孔子甚至讲过"未知生，焉知死" ❷。意思是说我们连人生诸事都没能弄清楚，怎么能弄明白人死后的事呢！不过，生于孔子之后的墨子却大肆宣扬上天和鬼神的存在，并极力渲染它们无所不能的神力。

墨子认为上天的意志是至高无上的，即使是天子也必须服从天意。他举了这样一个例子：如果天子生了病，会准备祭品向上天和神鬼祈祷，之后，上天就会去除他的病患。但是从来没有听说过上天会向天子祈祷的，所以说天要比天子尊贵。墨子不仅认为天有意志，还极力证明鬼神也是存在的。他首先引用《夏书》《商书》和《周书》上关于鬼神的记载，接着又举了一系列的例子：周宣王错杀杜伯，三年以后，杜伯的鬼魂将周宣王射死报仇；秦穆公有仁德，于是神人句芒白天现身，代表上天赐给穆公十九年的寿命；燕简公杀了无罪的庄子仪，后来庄子仪的鬼神前来复仇，将燕简公杀死在车上；宋文君时，一个祝人不遵守祭祀之法，结果被神杀死在祭坛上；齐国的两个大臣王里国与中里徼打官司，他们让神附体的羊来评判，结

---

❶《论语·述而》。
❷《论语·先进》。

❶ *Analects*, "Shu'er."
❷ *Analects*, "Xianjin."

was butted to death by the sheep. Through these instances Mozi verified to the people of the world that ghosts and spirits actually existed.

Well then, was Mozi actually a believer in God? After a close analysis, it is not hard to discover that when Mozi mentioned the "Will of Heaven," and stressed "Explaining Ghosts," he was only using a trick of setting up religion to teach the way of the spirits. As for his personal beliefs, Mozi himself did not really believe in the existence of Heaven or ghosts. He opposed lavish burials, opposed wasting large quantities of sacrificial offering used in making sacrifices; this demonstrates that he was not blindly prostrating himself to worship Heaven or ghosts. So this begs the question of "why did Mozi 'venerate Heaven and serve ghosts?'"

During his entire life Mozi travelled around campaigning, trying to persuade those above and teach those below; he strove to "stimulate benefits for all the world, and eradicate harmful things in the world." Nevertheless, he clearly realized that merely depending on propaganda and itinerary lecturing would be unable to cause men, especially the ruling class, to completely follow his political policies. Therefore he dredged up from the midst of the traditional culture the belief in the Heavenly God and ghosts and spirits, intending to draw strength from this supernatural and mystical power to restrain the ruling class, and thence achieve his ideals for saving the world. This is to say that Mozi's "Will of Heaven" and "Explaining Ghosts" merely drew on the externalities of the primitive belief in ghosts and spirits; its original nature however was a trick employed by Mozi to implement his ideal form of society and government. Mozi's "venerating Heaven and serving ghosts" was for the sake of drawing on the power of Heaven and ghosts to remake society and to govern the nation, that is, to draw on the authority of the Heavenly God and ghosts and spirits to implement his social and political ideals. In the final analysis, Mozi utilized Heaven and ghosts "to set up religion to teach the way of the spirits."

From Mozi's point of view, the will of Heaven was the ultimate authority, and it dominated all things in the world. All men in the world, regardless of whether poor or wealthy, noble or base, were his people; all remained under his protection and supervision. If one committed a crime again man, perhaps there was a place to hide; but if one committed a crime against Heaven, there was no place to hide. Since the will of Heaven was the highest authority, then from the Son of Heaven on down to the common people, all had to obey it. Then what after all was the will of Heaven? Mozi said, "Heaven desired justice and hated injustice." ❶ Heaven above hoped that the people would conduct themselves according to the standard of "justice," and oppose those who acted unjustly.

果中里徼被羊撞死。墨子通过这些事例向世人证明，鬼神的确是存在的。

那么，墨子是有神论者吗？我们仔细分析之后便不难发现，墨子讲"天志"、主"明鬼"，只不过是一种"神道设教"的手段而已。就墨子本人而言，他未必真正相信天、鬼的存在。他反对厚葬，反对浪费大量的祭品去祭祀，这表明他对天、鬼并不是盲目地顶礼膜拜。那墨子为什么还要"尊天事鬼"呢？

墨子一生奔走呼号、上说下教，致力于"兴天下之利，除天下之害"。然而他也清楚地知道，仅仅靠宣传游说，是无法让世人尤其是统治者完全信奉他的政治主张的。于是他从传统文化中发掘出天帝鬼神的信仰，意图借助这种超自然的神秘力量来约束统治者，从而实现其救世的理想。也就是说，墨子的"天志"、"明鬼"仅仅是借助了原始的鬼神信仰的外衣，其本质不过是推行墨子社会政治理想的手段而已。墨子"尊天事鬼"是为了借助天、鬼的力量来改造社会、治理国家，也即借助天帝鬼神的权威来推行其社会政治理想。说到底，墨子是利用天、鬼来"神道设教"。

在墨子看来，天的意志是至高无上的，他主宰着世间万物。普天之下的人们，无论贫富贵贱都是他的子民，都在他的庇佑和监视之下。如果获罪于人，也许有处可躲，若获罪于上天，则无处可逃。既然天的意志是至高无上的，那么上至天子下到庶民，都必须顺从天意。那么天的意志究竟是什么呢？墨子说："天欲义而恶不义。"❶上天希望人们按照"义"的标准行事，反对人们去做不义的事情。具体来说就是反对大国攻打小国，

---

❶《天志上》。

❶ "Will of Heaven," Part One.

Speaking more concretely, it meant opposing great states attacking small states, and large clans attacking small clans; it meant opposing the strong browbeating the weak and the masses deceiving the few. It meant hoping that men would be able to assist each other, and devote themselves to their jobs. The will of Heaven above clearly was the universal love, opposition to offensive warfare, identifying upwardly and being frugal in expenditures that Mozi advocated. Concerning this, the following passage is more explicit: "Those who conform to Heaven's will embrace universal love, join in acts of mutual benefit, and definitely will be rewarded. Those who oppose Heaven's will separately hate each other, join in mutual plundering, and certainly will be punished." ❶

Through Mozi's reinterpretation, "the will of Heaven above" became the will of Mozi. Because Mozi came from the lower class of society, what he proposed as "Universal Love," "Against Offensive Warfare," "Identifying with One's Superior" and "Frugal in Expenditures," all reflected the aspirations of the laboring class of people who had fully experienced the poverty associated with warfare. In this way, the will of Heaven above became the will of the laboring class of people. Heaven above completely divested itself of its coloration of mystery, and became the spokesman for the laboring class of people. Mozi's strenuously propagandized the awe and spiritual power of Heaven above out of the desire to draw on the authority of Heaven above to reward good and punish evil, to stimulate benefit and eradicate harm, to save a chaotic world, to enable society to be stable and friendly and the people to live in peace and work in happiness.

Sharing the same goal as "Venerating Heaven," Mozi's "Serving the Spirits" also attempted to draw on the power of ghosts and spirits to sell his own theories. In "Explaining Ghosts," Part Two, he clearly stated the purpose by explaining that at the present time of unalloyed chaos was prevalent due to warfare, lords were not kind, ministers were not loyal, fathers were not compassionate, sons were not filial, those in office did not strive to manage the state, and the commoners did not strive to engage in production; in seeking the reason for all of this, it is found in people doubting the existence of ghosts and spirits. Mozi did not spare any effort to explain the accounts of ghosts and spirits found in the historical records to the people and to share legends concerning them. His purpose was the desire to verify the actual existence of ghosts and spirits. Not only this, ghosts and spirits also looked down on every move made by people of the world. If someone performed good deeds, they would certainly be rewarded by them; if people acted wickedly, they would

大家攻打小家；反对恃强凌弱、以众欺寡；希望人们能互相帮助，努力工作。上天的意志分明就是墨子所主张的兼爱、非攻、尚同和节用，对此，下面这段文字说得更为明显："顺天意者，兼相爱、交相利，必得赏；反天意者，别相恶、交相贼，必得罚。" ❶

经过墨子的一番改造，"上天的意志"就变成了墨子的意志。由于墨子出身于社会下层，他所提倡的"兼爱"、"非攻"、"尚同"、"尚贤"、"节用"等主张，都是饱经战乱贫困之苦的劳动人民的愿望。这样，上天的意志就变成了劳动人民的意志。上天脱尽了原来的神秘色彩，成为劳动人民的代言人。墨子极力宣扬上天的威严和神力，就是想借助上天的权威来赏善罚恶、兴利除害，拯救乱世，使社会能够安定和睦，人民能够安居乐业。

与"尊天"的目的一样，墨子"事鬼"也是企图借助鬼神的力量来推销他的学说。在《明鬼下》篇中，他开宗明义地说，当今天下战乱频繁，君不惠、臣不忠，父不慈、子不孝，当官的不努力治理国家，老百姓不努力从事生产，盗贼横行，究其原因，都在于人们怀疑鬼神的存在。墨子不厌其烦地向人们讲述史书中有关鬼神的记载以及关于鬼神的传闻，目的就是想证明鬼神确实是存在的。不仅如此，鬼神还监视着世人的一举一动。如果有人行善一定会得到鬼神的赏赐，如果有人做恶也必

---

❶《天志上》。

❶ "Will of Heaven," Part One.

certainly be punished by them. In order to make the ruling class receptive of his thought, Mozi also recounted positively the deeds of the ancient sages such as Yao, Shun, Yu, and Kings Wen and Wu of Zhou. Because all of them "venerated and served the ghosts and spirits," not only were they rewarded by Heaven above and established the foundation of a state for a thousand ages, they moreover were lavishly praised by men of later ages. But such tyrants as Jie and Zhou on the other hand, due to "disgracing Heaven and shaming the ghosts," were punished by Heaven above, and not only lost their kingdoms but also left shameful reputations down the ages.

Among all of the pre-Qin philosophers, Mozi took a clear-cut stand to advocate the "Will of Heaven" and "Explaining Ghosts." Doesn't this mean then that Mozi was a religious leader? Doesn't this mean that Mohism was a religious sect? Concerning this question, scholarly debate is varied and voluble, and unable to reach a consensus. Guo Moruo felt that Mozi was a religious founder in the manner of Jesus or Mohammed. In his *General History of China*, Bai Shouyi said, "Mozi founded the academic school of Mohism. This was an institution that possessed organization and discipline with a political nature that still carried with it the coloration of a religion." ❶ Such scholars as Xu Fuguan, Tan Jiajian and Cai Renhou, et al., instead advocated the view that Mohism was not a religious organization. Viewed from its content, Mozi took a clear-cut stand to propagandize "venerating Heaven and serving the spirits;" and the Mohist school was a strictly organized and disciplined school among the people led by a leader called a grandmaster that assuredly was similar at various points to a religious organization. But in general religions have a heavy coloration of mysticism, and religious founders often claim to possess limitless supernatural powers, let alone the fact that what religions seek in general are blessings from the beyond or in the next world. Yet during his entire life, Mozi strove diligently to eliminate the bitter suffering of the people and establish a just and righteous society in which all helped and loved each other, just as the saying goes of "wearing yourself out in the service of others." In addition to this, Mozi's entire series of proposals all targeted the social ills, and took their points of departure from social reality. This is to say that Mozi's theories did not seek to lead men to an unknown and mysterious world, but at every point was concerned with reality and the active reformation of society. Therefore, Mohism seemed to be a religion yet actually was not a religion.

Although Mohism was not a religious organization, Mozi maintained the religious hue of the "Will of Heaven" and "Explaining Ghosts;" this thought

然会遭到鬼神的惩罚。为了让统治者能够接受他的思想，墨子还称述了古代圣王如尧、舜、禹、周文王、周武王的事迹。他们都因为"尊天事鬼"，不但得到了上天的赏赐，建立万世基业，而且深受后人赞誉；而桀、纣等暴君则因为"诟天侮鬼"，结果受到上天的惩罚，不但江山不保，而且遗臭万年。

在先秦诸子中，墨子旗帜鲜明地主张"天志"、"明鬼"，那么墨子是不是一个宗教家？墨家学派是不是一个宗教教派呢？关于这个问题，学者们众说纷纭、莫衷一是。郭沫若就认为墨子是一个像耶稣、穆罕默德一样的教主。白寿彝在《中国通史》中说："墨子创立了墨家学派。这是一个有组织纪律，具有政治性质而带有宗教色彩的团体。"❶徐复观、谭家健、蔡仁厚等学者则主张墨家学派不是宗教团体。从内容来看，墨子旗帜鲜明地宣扬"尊天事鬼"，墨家学派是一个以巨子为首的、有着严明的组织纪律的民间团体，确实与宗教组织有几分相似。但是宗教一般都带有浓厚的神秘色彩，而且创教者本人往往以法力无边的教主自居，再加上宗教所追求的一般都是超世的或来世的幸福。而墨子一生孜孜以求的是消除人民的苦难，建立一个互助互爱、公平正义的社会，即所谓"摩顶放踵利天下，为之"。此外，墨子的一系列主张，无不针对社会弊端而发，无不立足社会现实。也就是说，墨子的学说不是将人们引向未知的神秘世界，而是处处关注现实，积极改造社会。因此，墨家貌似宗教而实非宗教。

虽然墨家不是宗教组织，但墨子带有宗教色彩的"天志"、"明鬼"思想却对中国的道教产生了深远的影响。道教也将天

---

❶ 白寿彝：《中国通史》第四册，上海人民出版社，1994年，第1150页。

❶ Bai Shouyi, *General History of China*, Vol. 4, Shanghai People's Publishing House, 1994, p. 1150.

created a profound and wide influence on Chinese Taoism. Taoism also regarded Heaven as the supreme power of the universe. However what Mozi meant by Heaven was an invisible supernatural spiritual force, while Taoists personified Heaven as the "Heavenly Lord." Mozi regarded the will of Heaven as the standard against which to measure all right and wrong, and good and evil, and considered Heaven to be the supreme arbiter of the human realm, and the Taoist early canon the *Scripture of Great Peace* also taught this. In the *Scripture of Great Peace*, it says, "Heaven is impartial in dispensing blessings; it blesses whoever is sincere" and "Heaven reflects human conduct the same as would a mirror." ❶ This remarkably expressed the justice embodied in Heaven above as the arbiter of the human realm. If the people contravened the will of Heaven, then they would meet with the punishment of Heaven above: "If you gain the will of Heaven, you will enjoy long-term good fortune; if you go against it, then flood, drought and other aspects of the weather will turn perverse; calamities will pile up and strange prodigies will break out without cessation. Call them natural disasters and unusual phenomena." ❷ This should be compared to *Mozi*, "Identifying with One's Superior," Part Two: "If Heaven changes the seasons of hot and cold, snow and frost fall out of season, the five crops do not ripen, the six types of domesticated animals are not husbanded, natural disasters and plagues break out, whirlwinds blast and torrential rains fall; these come in succession as punishments sent down by Heaven." In comparing these two passages, it is not hard to discover that they share similarities. Hence the *Scripture of Great Peace* is the same as the *Mozi* in interpreting natural disasters as functioning as a kind of warning from Heaven directed towards the incorrect behavior of people. From this it can be seen that the thought of early Taoism on "Heaven responds with Heaven's might" can be traced to the same line of thinking as Mozi's "Heaven watches over and the ghosts punish." Not only this, but the thinking of religious Taoism's "inherit the blessings and burdens of (ancestors who either followed or disobeyed) the Heavenly way" and "eliminate a pre-ordered lifespan and reduce one's years (due to evil conduct)" share the same source.

作为宇宙间的最高主宰。只不过墨子所讲的天是无形的，拥有超自然的神力，而道教却将天人格化为"天君"。墨子把天的意志作为衡量一切是非善恶的标准，把天当作世间的最高裁决者，而道教早期经典《太平经》也是如此。《太平经》中说："天无私祜，祜之有信"，"天之照人，与镜无异" ❶，突出表现了上天作为世间裁决者的公正性。人们如果违背天意，就会遭到上天的惩罚，"得天心意，如长吉。逆之则水旱气乖忤，流灾积成，变怪不可止，名为灾异。" ❷ 如果将其与《墨子·尚同中》的"当若天降寒热不节，雪霜雨露不时，五谷不孰，六畜不遂，疾灾戾疫，飘风苦雨，荐臻而至者，此天之降罚也"进行对比，就不难发现二者的之间相似性。《太平经》也和《墨子》一样，认为自然灾害是上天对人们错误行为的一种警示。由此可见，早期道教"天应天威"的思想与墨子"天监鬼罚"的思想可以说是一脉相承。不仅如此，道教中的"天道承负"和"除算减年"也与墨家的"天监鬼罚"有着一定的渊源关系。

❶ 王明：《太平经合校》，中华书局，1960年，第18页。
❷ 王明：《太平经合校》，中华书局，1960年，第178页。

❶ Wang Ming, *Combined Corrections to the Scripture of Great Peace*, Zhonghua Book Co., 1960, p. 18.
❷ Ibid, p. 178.

春秋时代的普通服装

An Ordinary Garment in the Spring and Autumn Period

十 强教强学，言传身教

——墨家的教育思想

Chapter X Powerful Teaching and Powerful Learning, Practicing What He Preached: Mozi's Educational Thought

After Mozi discovered the defects in Confucianism, he decided to "turn against the way of the Zhou and utilize the policies of Xia." ❶ He no longer revered the way of the Zhou or esteemed the rites and music; instead he changed to travelling around in all sorts of terrible conditions, emulating the spirit of Yu of Xia. However, Mozi knew that during that age of blood and fire, personal strength was like a drop in the ocean, and was completely useless in shouldering the great burden of saving the people and in stimulating benefits to the world. In "Questions from Lu," Mozi explained the limitations of personal strength: After a person personally sows a crop, even if his harvest is good, he cannot feed the people of the world; even if each person received a peck of rice, it would still be impossible to insure that all the poor people of the world no longer suffer from hunger. Only by developing distinguished men such as himself can all strive together and be truly able to establish an ideal society where the government is flourishing and the people at peace, where mutual help and universal love prevails.

In Mozi's heart of hearts, a distinguished men was known as a "universal knight." In "Universal Love," Part Two, "when you see hungry persons, then give them something to eat; when you see cold persons, give them something to wear; when you see sick persons, then take care of them; when you see dead persons, then bury them." Regardless of the time or place, when necessary Mohists must boldly step forward without hesitation to sacrifice the self to benefit others.

Because of this, Mozi regarded education as an important means for achieving an ideal society. He not only demanded that "those with the strength be anxious to aid others, those with the means strive to share with others," but that one must even more so demand that "enlightened persons should teach others diligently." He felt that when silent one could reflect; when speaking one could teach others; when acting one could actively achieve things. When these three things are engaged in at appropriate times, then one is able to become a sage. "Teaching others" is one quality that must be present for becoming a sage; it is evident that education plays a decisive role for Mozi in his heart of hearts.

Therefore, Mozi accepted students on a broad scale, and implemented Confucius's own dictum of "teaching without regard to class" even more comprehensively than Confucius himself. Confucius required that "anyone who would present anything equal or above dried meat would be taught without exception;" ❷ but he required ten strips of dried meat as tuition, before he would be willing to bequeath his teachings. But for the poor people, strips

墨子在发现儒学弊端之后，决定"背周道而用夏政"❶，不再崇周道、尚礼乐，改以追求栉风沐雨、一绳天下的夏禹精神。但是墨子知道，在那个血与火的时代，个人的力量只是沧海一粟，根本无法承担拯救苍生、兴利天下的重担。在《鲁问》中墨子道出了个人力量的有限性：一个人亲自耕种，就算收成很好，把自己的粮食分给天下人，每个人也得不到一升粟米；即使能得到一升粟米，也无法让全天下的穷人不再忍饥挨饿。只有培养出与自己一样的贤士，大家共同努力，才能真正建立起一个政兴人和、互助兼爱的理想社会。

墨子心目当中的贤士被称作"兼士"，《兼爱下》中记载他们"看到饥饿的人就给他们饭吃，看到寒冷的人就给他们衣服穿，看到有病的人就照顾他们，看到去世的人就埋葬他们"。无论何时何地，在必要的时候他们都能毫不犹豫地挺身而出，损己以利人。

墨子因此把教育当作实现自己社会理想的重要手段，他不仅要求"有力者疾以助人，有财者勉以分人"，更要求"有道者劝以教人"。他认为沉默的时候能够自己思考，说话的时候能够教诲他人，行动的时候能够积极做事，这三者交替进行，就能成为圣人。"教诲他人"是成为圣人必备的素质之一，可见教育在墨子心目中的地位举足轻重。

因此，墨子广收门徒，将孔子"有教无类"的主张贯彻得更加彻底。孔子要求"自行束脩以上，吾未尝无诲焉"❷，必须送十条干肉做学费，他才愿意给予教诲。但对于贫民而言，

---

❶《淮南子·要略》。
❷《论语·述而》。

❶ *Huainanzi*, "Yaolue."
❷ *Analects*, "Shu'er."

of dried meat doubtlessly would be considered a luxury. Mozi did not require any material stipulation, and Mozi never refused anyone who sought him out as a teacher, truly embodying the thought of equal opportunity education. For those who did not seek to progress, Mozi still took the initiative in enlightening and encouraging them to study.

One young student travelled to study under Mozi and stood in front of his gate, his appearance heroic and uncommon, quite out of the ordinary; moreover he was endowed with natural intelligence and a quick mind. But this person was not fond of study, and liked to loaf around idling all day. So Mozi said to him, "Study with me, and afterward I will recommend you for office." After the student heard this, he was quite pleased, and agreed to follow Mozi as a student. After a year, the youth felt that he had already finished his studies, thereupon he requested an office from Mozi. Mozi said, "I am unable to recommend you for office." The youth immediately fell into a towering rage, and hotly questioned Mozi why he would go back on his word. Mozi did not immediately answer his question; instead he shared a story from the state of Lu. Once five brothers lost their father in death; the eldest son drank wine every day and was not willing to bury his father. His four younger brothers said to him, "Come with us to bury our father, and we will buy some wine for you." After the burial, the eldest son asked his younger brothers for wine. They, however, said, "We won't give you any wine. You buried your father, and we buried our father. How can it be that our father was not your father? If you did not bury your father, others would ridicule you, so we used the pretext of buying wine to deceive you to bury our father." After sharing this story, Mozi got back to the subject at hand and told the youth, "Now your studies are for the sake of performing righteous deeds, and my studies are towards the same ends; is it the case that only I should perform righteous deeds? I have urged you to study also to prevent others from ridiculing you!" After the youth heard this, he at last realized the truth, and lowered his head in shame.

On another occasion Mozi asked another person who had come to visit, saying, "Why don't you study?" That person answered, "It is because no one in my extended family loves to study." Mozi counseled him, "Your attitude is erroneous. How could it be that one who loved beauty would not love beauty unless somebody in his family loved beauty? How could it be that one who pursued wealth and honor would not pursue them unless somebody in his family pursued them? Those who love beauty and those who pursue wealth and honor strive after them regardless of what others do. Performing righteous deeds is a grand thing to do in the world. Why should you first see what others

十条干肉无疑也是一种奢侈品。而墨子则不讲任何物质条件，对于前来求学的弟子，墨子来者不拒，真正体现了教育机会均等的思想。而对于那些不求上进之人，墨子还会主动启发、劝导他们学习。

有一个游学于墨子门下的年轻人，长得英武不凡、一表人才，而且天资聪颖、才思敏捷，但这个人却不爱学习，整日游手好闲。墨子便对他说："你跟着我学习吧，学成之后我举荐你当官。"年轻人听后十分高兴，同意跟随墨子学习。一年后，年轻人认为自己已经学有所成，于是向墨子求官。墨子却说："我不能举荐你做官。"年轻人顿时火冒三丈，质问墨子为什么言而无信。墨子并没有立即回答他的问题，而是讲了鲁国的一个故事：有兄弟五人，他们的父亲去世了，长子天天喝酒不愿意埋葬父亲。他的四个弟弟说："你和我们一起把父亲埋了，我们就给你买酒。"埋完后，长子向弟弟们讨酒，弟弟们却说："我们不会给你酒的。你埋你的父亲，我们埋我们的父亲，难道我们的父亲不是你的父亲吗？你若不埋葬父亲，别人就会讥笑你，所以我们才用买酒的谎言骗你埋葬了父亲。"讲完故事，墨子言归正传，告诉年轻人："现在你学习是为了行义，我学习也是为了行义，难道只应该我一个人行义吗？我劝你学习，也是为了防止别人讥笑你呀！"年轻人听后终于醒悟过来，羞愧地低下了头。

还有一次，墨子问一个前来拜访他的人："你怎么不学习呢？"那人回答说："因为我的家族里没有人爱学习。"墨子劝导他："你这样的想法可不对啊！爱美之人，难道会因为他的家族中没有人爱美，他就不爱美了吗？追求富贵的人，难道会因为他家族的人都不追求富贵，他就不追求了吗？爱美之人与追求富贵的人，不管别人如何，他们都会努力去做。行义是天

are doing before striving to perform them?" After that person listened to Mozi's words, he was convinced in his mind and repeatedly nodded his head stating that it was true.

Confucians, the founders of private education, advocated "Ritual requires that one comes seeking learning, it has never been heard that one sets out to teach," ❶ and "Those who set off are not pursued, and those who come are not rejected." ❷ Mozi took an additional step and not only accepted "those who came," toward those who "set off" he took the initiative in offering to teach them. The "Questions of Lu" recorded the following story: In the southern part of Lu there was a peasant named Wu Lü; during the winter he manufactured pottery vessels, and in the summer he was busy in the agrarian lifestyle, and regarded himself as a worthy comparable to Shun. After Mozi heard of him he set off to pay him a visit. When Wu Lü saw Mozi, he said to him, "How is it necessary to talk about the matter of doing good deeds?" Mozi said to him, "Suppose no one in the world knew the methods of plowing; who do you suppose would achieve the greatest merit, he who taught others how to plow or he who just worried about his own plowing and did not teach others to plow?" Wu Lü answered, "Of course the one who taught others how to plow achieved the greatest merit." Then Mozi continued, saying, "Suppose you were going to attack an unrighteous state and one sent the officers and troops charging ahead to the sound of drums to bravely kill the enemy and one sent the officers and troops charging on to kill the enemy without the sound of drums, which one would achieve the greatest merit?" "Of course it is the one who sounded the drums whose merit was the greatest." After hearing Wu Lüs response, Mozi again spoke, saying, "Now there are few in the world who know about righteousness, and those who teach them how to do good works achieve great merit, so why not teach them? If you are able to sound a drum and summon the people of the world to come and do good deeds, would not the righteousness that I teach spread even more widely?"

Mozi advocated that "in every case explain things from the point of view of the people," only fearing that "If one does not explain things forcedly, then people would not understand." ❸ This type of "teaching forcedly" in terms of pedagogical principles during pre-Qin times can be said to have been unique for the time. In order to do this, Mozi held a famous debate with the great Confucian master Gongmeng. Gongmengzi felt that teaching students should be like striking a bell, "If you strike it, it will boom; if you do not strike it, it will not boom." ❹ If students did not inquire of themselves, then there was no need to actively seek to teach them. At this point he then ridiculed Mozi, "Who

下的大事，何必先看别人怎样再努力去做呢？"那人听了墨子的话，心悦诚服，频频点头称是。

私学开创者儒家提倡"礼闻来学，不闻往教"❶、"往者不追，来者不拒"❷，墨子则更进一步，不仅接受"来者"，对于"往者"还主动送教上门。在《鲁问》篇中就记载了一个这样的故事：鲁国南部有一个名叫吴虑的农夫，冬天制造陶器，夏天忙于农活，自己将自己比作和舜一样的贤人，墨子听说后专程前往拜见。吴虑见到墨子后对他说："行义这样的事哪里用得着嘴上说呢？"墨子对他说："假设天下人都不知道耕作的方法，教别人如何耕作的人和只顾自己耕作不教别人的人，哪一个的功劳更大呢？"吴虑答道："当然是教别人耕作方法的人更有功劳。"墨子接着说："假设要去攻打不义之国，鸣鼓而使众多士兵奋勇杀敌的人和不鸣鼓而使众多的士兵杀敌的人，哪个人的功劳更大？""当然是鸣鼓的人功劳更大。"听到吴虑的回答，墨子又说道："现在天下的百姓知道义的少，教他们如何行义的人功劳很大，为什么不教他们呢？如果能鸣鼓号召天下人都来行义，我的义不就传播得更广了吗？"

墨子主张"遍从人而说之"，唯恐"不强说人，人莫之知也"❸。这种"强教"于人的教学原则在先秦可谓独树一帜，为此，墨子还和儒家大师公孟子进行过一场著名的辩论。公孟子认为，教育学生应该像敲钟一样，"扣则鸣，不扣则不鸣"❹，如果学生不问自己，就不必主动去教。他就此嘲笑墨

---

❶《礼记·曲礼上》。
❷《孟子·尽心下》。
❸《公孟》。
❹《公孟》。

❶ *Records of the Ritualists*, "Quli," Part One.
❷ *Mencius*, "Jinxin," Part Two.
❸ "Gongmeng."
❹ "Gongmeng."

would not hear about a person who truly performed good deeds? It is just like a piece of beautiful jade hidden away out of sight still being able to spread an unusual luster. It is also just like a beautiful woman who is hidden away out of sight, yet those who seek her hand are numberless. If one day she bragged about herself, then no one would seek her hand! Now you wander around all over the place persuading the people, proclaiming your own theories; is it necessary to belabor yourself to such an extent?" Mozi refuted him, saying, "Now society is chaotic and unsettled; there are many who seek beautiful women; even if they lie hidden away from view, many will step forward to seek her hand. But now those who are seeking the good are too few; if I do not strive to exhort others, then they will not understand the principle of seeking the good." In *Zhuangzi*, "The World," it says that Mozi "wandered the world over, trying to persuade those above and teach those below. Even when he was not accepted in the world, he was forceful and raucous, and never gave up." What was praised was Mozi's active effort at education and unyielding spirit of teaching.

Another important reason for Mozi to venerate education to such an extent and to actively strive to encourage learning was that he felt that the moral character of a man's thought would be influenced by the bad habits of his environment. If one were to take a piece of unbleached white silk and toss it into a dyeing vat, "if it were dyed blue, then it would be blue; if it were dyed yellow, then it would be yellow." ❶ Sighing with emotion over this, Mozi thought about men in their actual living environments and felt that environment was a type of dyeing vat; being properly influenced, one could then become an overlord and gain high rank in the world. Being improperly influenced would lead to the destruction of the state and of the individual, and lead to becoming the object of ridicule in the world. According to how Mozi viewed things, what leads to men becoming evil in an age when social morals are declining daily, is not that men are born evil, but that they are contaminated by bad practices. Because the goodness or evil in men is due to acquired habits, one must actively teach and transform them before society can be reformed.

With regard to the content of education, Mozi smashed through the protective screen of the Confucian "Six Skills" of ritual, music, archery, chariot driving, calligraphy and mathematics, and acted according to the principle of "transmit what was good anciently, enact what is good at the present time." ❷ According to the actual conditions of social production, he established some new contents for education, and actively expanded the scope

子："真正行善的人，谁人不知呢？好比美玉深藏不露，仍能绽放异彩。好比美女隐而不出，依然追求者众多。一旦她自我炫耀，人们就不会娶她了。现在你到处跟人家游说，宣讲自己的主张，有必要这么辛劳吗！"墨子反驳道："现在社会动乱不安，追求美女的人多，即使她们隐而不出，也会有很多人前来求娶。而现在追求善的人太少了，如果不努力劝说，他们就不会懂得求善的道理。"《庄子·天下》篇中说墨子"周行天下，上说下教；虽天下不取，强聒而不舍者也"。所称赞的就是墨子的这种积极施教，矢志不渝的教学精神。

墨子如此重视教育、积极努力地劝学，还有一个重要原因，那就是他认为人的思想品格会受到环境习染的影响。将一块白净的"素丝"丢入染缸之中，"染于苍则苍，染于黄则黄"❶。感慨于此，墨子联想到对于生活在现实环境之中的人来说，环境也是一只染缸，受到的熏染得当，就能成就霸业，显荣于天下；受到的熏染不得当，就会过国破身亡，被天下人耻笑。在墨子看来，导致当时世风日下的恶人们并非天生就是恶人，而是沾染了社会上的不良习气。因为人的善恶都是后天习染造成的，所以必须积极地教化才能有效地改良社会。

在教育内容方面，墨子突破儒家礼、乐、射、御、书、数这"六艺"的藩篱，按照"古之善者则述之，今之善者则作之"❷的原则，根据当时社会生产的实际需要，创设了一些新的教学内容，极大地扩展了教学范围。墨子将教育内容大致分为"谈辩"、"说书"、"从事"三个方面。《耕柱》篇中说："能

---

❶《所染》。
❷《耕柱》。

❶ "On Dyeing."
❷ "Geng Zhu."

of education. Mozi basically divided the content of education into the three divisions of "discussion and debate," "explaining writings" and "engaging in action." In the "Geng Zhu" it says, "He who can discuss and debate should discuss and debate; he who can explain writings should explain writings; he who can engage in action should engage in action." "Discussion and debate" refers to learning how to talk or the methods and skills of debate; the purpose was to nurture the persuaders and roaming scholarly debaters needed by the society of the time. "Explaining writings" indicates learning the theories and principles contained in books, and to promulgate the knowledge of culture and science; the purpose is to nurture missionaries to take a further step in disseminating the teachings of the Mohist sect. "Engaging in action" indicates learning the practical skills associated with industry, agriculture, business and weapons manufacturing to nurture specialists to engage in the various types of practical production.

Mozi deeply realized that men each enjoyed different natural endowments, and so he needed to teach in accordance with each man's special aptitude. Therefore, he divided the content of his own education into three aspects, in order to teach each according to his individual talents. Among them, the discipline of "engaging in action" can be said to have a distinctive style.

We know that Mozi and many of the disciples whom he recruited all came from among the common people; additionally, many of them were craftsmen, and some even came from among the so-called "base" people. Therefore, Mozi completely emphasized the teaching of production skills and the knowledge of natural science. In the course of his teaching, he and his disciples never departed from production activities. Instead, through summarizing the experiences gained from putting production into action, they ceaselessly proposed some valuable knowledge rich in scientific value, and fused this knowledge into their teaching. This formed a fresh contrast to Confucian private education which did not emphasize the study of "physical implements." Once Confucius berated his student Fan Chi, who wanted to study agriculture for being a "petty person," he himself being one who "never moved his four limbs" and "can't distinguish the five crops." ❶

The disciples who pursued the discipline of engaging in action in the main studied production techniques and military skills, engaged in the techniques of woodworking and other such physical labor or military oriented trades to help the various feudal princes to protect cities and defend the land. They personally participated in production, manufactured implements for military use, accumulating rich experiences in production. They not only transformed this

谈辩者谈辩，能说书者说书，能从事者从事。""谈辩"指学习谈话、论辩的方法和技巧，目的是为了培养当时社会所需要的说客和游士；"说书"指学习书本中的理论和原理，传授文化科学知识，目的是为了培养可以进一步传道的本派传人；春秋时期的陶罐"从事"指学习工业、农业、商业、兵器制造中的实际技能，以培养可以从事各种生产实践的专门人才。

墨子深知人的秉赋各不相同，必须根据个人的特点因材施教。所以，他将自己的教育内容分成了以上三个方面，因其才而教之。其中，"从事"一科在先秦私学教育中可以说是别具一格。

我们知道，墨子和墨子招收的许多弟子都出身平民，有许多成员是手工业者，还有一些"贱民"。因此，墨子十分重视生产技能和自然科学知识的教授。他和他的弟子们在教学过程并不脱离生产活动，反而通过对生产实践中经验的总结，不断提出一些富有科学价值的知识，并把这些知识融入教学之中。这与孔门私学不注重"形下之器"的学习形成了鲜明的对比。孔子曾骂想学农耕的学生樊迟为"小人"，自己也"四体不勤，五谷不分"❶。

从事科的弟子主要学习生产技术和军事技艺，从事工匠技艺等体力劳动或在战争帮助诸侯守城卫地。他们亲自参与生产，制作军事器械，积累了丰富的生产经验，并将之上升到理论高

❶《论语·微子》。

❶ *Analects*, "Weizi."

experience into lofty theories, but also knew how things were, and why things were the way they were. In the course of Chinese educational history, the influence exerted by this type of educational content was of extreme depth and width. This is precisely what Wu Ni said in her *Research into Various Issues in the Development of Private Education in Ancient China*: "The lack of education in technical knowledge was a perennial and great defect in ancient Chinese education; however, the content and methods of private education in technical knowledge and experimentation that Mozi created founded the precursor of technical education in ancient China. After Mozi, private education in science and technology seemed to be a single spark of light that was transmitted and maintained through private education, which at certain times appeared in education as learning in science and technology." ❶ In the main, content of this type was recorded in four sections of the *Mozi*, "Canon," Part One, "Canonical Explanations," Part One, "Canon," Part Two, and "Canonical Explanations," Part Two as well as eleven sections in "Preparing City Gates." The content may be regarded as all-embracing, broad and profound; it included knowledge of such scientific realms as mathematics, mechanics, astronomy and machine manufacturing.

In addition to teaching according to the aptitudes of students, Mozi's pedagogy was permeated with the principle of "teaching according to capacity," and refused to engage in such activities as "piling it on in teaching" those students who lacked the ability to learn. "Gongmeng" recorded the story of several students who desired to learn archery being dissuaded by Mozi. Several disciples reported to Mozi that they wanted to learn archery. Mozi said, "You cannot. Clever people need to determine their own abilities before trying to do something. Brave knights of national repute who want to do battle as well as help others find it impossible to do both, so how can the normal student do well in his studies and also learn archery?" Mozi was obviously one to teach according to a student's capacity, and would never aim too high.

Although in terms of pedagogical principle and the content of education Mozi was not entirely similar to Confucians, as for the moral cultivation of students, both schools were quite similar. It says in the *Analects*, "Shu'er" : "Set your will on the Way, base yourself on virtue, act according to humanness, and wander amid the various skills." Mozi also felt that a truly worthy man, in addition to being "discerning in speech, and erudite in the techniques of the way," also had to be "good at moral conduct." ❷ Therefore, he highly emphasized the moral training of his disciples. First of all, he demanded of his

度，不仅知其然，而且知其所以然。这样的教育内容在中国古代教育史上影响极为深远，正如吴霓在《中国古代私学发展诸问题研究》中所说："科技知识教育之缺乏一直是中国古代教育的一大缺陷，但是，墨子私学所创造的科技知识和实验的教学内容、方法，开创了古代科技教育的先河，墨子之后，科技私学似星星之火，一直在私家教育中传播着、延续着，并一度在官方教育中也出现过科技知识的教育。"❶这部分内容主要记录在《墨子》的《经上》、《经说上》、《经下》、《经说下》四篇以及《备城门》中讲守御的十一篇内容之中。其内容可谓包罗万象，博大精深，包含有数学、力学、光学、天文学、机械制造等多个学科领域的知识。

除了因材施教，墨子还在教学中对学生贯彻"量力而教"的原则，对那些并不具备能力的学生"过量而学"的行为予以阻止。《公孟》就记载了几个想学射箭的学生被墨子劝阻的故事：几个弟子禀告墨子想要学习射箭，墨子说："不可以。聪明的人必定衡量了自己的能力然后再去做事。国家级的勇士要想一边战斗，一边搀扶别人，尚且无法做到，普通的学生怎么能既学好学业又学好射箭呢？"墨子就是这样教导学生量力而学，决不能好高骛远。

虽然在教育原则和教育内容上，墨家与儒家不尽相同，但在学生的道德培养方面，两家却颇为一致。《论语·述而》中说："志于道，据于德，依于仁，游于艺。"墨子也认为真正的贤士除了"辩乎言谈，博乎道术"之外，还必须做到"厚乎德行"❷，因此他对弟子的道德情操培养也极为重视。他要求学

---

❶ 参见陈雪良：《墨子答客问》，上海人民出版社，1997年，第190页。
❷《尚贤上》。

❶ See Chen Xueliang, *Mozi Responding to Questions from Visitors*, Shanghai People's Publishing House, 1997, p. 190.
❷ "Elevating the Worthy," Part One.

students that they "live up to their words, and produce results in their actions." ❶ He absolutely opposed actions in which deeds did not come up to words. It said in "Gongmeng" that "when the mouth uttered something, the body must carry it out," meaning that the words which are spoken must be put into practice.

Mozi demanded this of his students, and demanded this of himself. As with all of his theories, he always personally observed them, taking the lead in putting them into practice. What he advocated concerning "frugality in usage" was an appeal "encouraging agriculture and being frugal in government expenditures." Therefore, he himself merely "ate according to his appetite, and wore clothes according to his size," leading a lofty but impoverished life. His advocacy of the theory of "universal love" stressed broad and impartial love; he therefore led his students in wandering day and night, performing good deeds in all directions. Under his personal example, Mohists wore coarse clothing and short jackets, ate simple fare and "never rested day or night, working themselves to the bone." ❷

Mozi not only demanded the unity of word and deed of his disciples, he also took the additional step of proposing the moral method of observation based on the "unity of motivation and result." ❸ One must not only look at what students do, but must look at the reason why they are doing it; that is, it is necessary to examine the moral conduct of students from the combined aspects of motivation for action and the results of the action. In the section "Questions from Lu" it records the following story: The Lord of Lu asked Mozi, "I have two sons, one who likes to study and one who likes to share his money and property with others. To whom should I make my heir?" Mozi said, "It is impossible to decide; perhaps they act this way to gain a good reputation. Those who fish are very respectful but not for the sake of bestowing a favor on the fish, and those who use poisoned biscuits to feed to rats do so not out of love for them. I hope you can observe them from the combined perspectives of their motivations and their results."

In addition to knowledge-based and moral-based education, Mozi also strongly emphasized teaching students learning methods. Mozi divided the sources of knowledge into "hearing, speech and personal." Knowledge gained from what others have transmitted is "hearing;" knowledge that traverses space and is gained through inference is "speech;" knowledge that is gained through the observations and experiences of the sense organs is "personal." Mozi felt that learning cannot stop at the direct knowledge gained through the senses and from others; what was more important was to be able to

生首先做到"言必信、行必果"❶，极力反对言行不一的行为。《公孟》篇还说："口言之，身必行之"，说出来的话就必须履行。

墨子是这样要求学生的，也是这样要求自己的。对于自己提出的理论，他总是身体力行，带头实施。他提出"节用"的主张，呼吁强本节用，于是自己"量腹而食，度身而衣"，过着十分清贫的生活。他提出"兼爱"学说，倡导广泛而无差别的爱，于是带领弟子日夜奔走，四处行义。在他的言传身教下，墨家弟子穿的是粗布短袄，吃的是粗劣的饭菜，"日夜不休，以自苦为极"❷。

墨子不仅要求学生言行合一，还进一步提出"合其志功而观"❸的道德考察方式。不仅要看学生做了什么，还要看学生为什么这样做，也就是从做事的动机和行事的效果两方面综合考核学生的道德行为。《鲁问》篇中曾记载过这样一个故事：鲁国国君问墨子："我有两个儿子，一个喜欢学习，一个喜欢把自己的钱财分给别人，我该让哪个做太子呢？"墨子说："这无法确定。或许他们是为了获得好名声才做这些事的。钓鱼的人那么恭敬，不是为了给鱼恩赐；用毒饼来喂老鼠，也不是因为爱它们。我希望您结合他们的动机和结果来考察。"

除了知识和道德教育，墨子还十分注重教授学生学习方法。墨子把知识的来源分为三类："闻、说、亲"。通过他人传递而得到知识，是"闻"；超越空间、通过推理而得到的知识，是"说"；通过感觉器官观察体验而得到的知识，是"亲"。墨子

❶《兼爱下》。
❷《庄子·天下》。
❸《鲁问》。

❶ "Universal Love," Part Two.
❷ *Zhuangzi*, "The World."
❸ "Questions from Lu."

think critically, to deduce, and to verify such knowledge, and gain indirect knowledge through these means. He transmitted these methods of cognitive learning to his students, and helped them to internalize them until they were learning skills inherent in each student, and thus achieved even better pedagogical results. It is precisely like the saying of "Giving a man a fish is not as good as teaching him to fish." It was because of mastering learning methodologies that Mohists and later Mohists never ceased to invent and innovate, impelling Mohism to an even higher pinnacle.

Under the inspiration of Mozi's personal example of teaching and great character, disciples of Mohism all were able "to tread on fire and never shirk in the face of death" in order to do good deeds. According to the account of "Equipping With Ladders," Qin Huali followed Mozi for three years, his hands and feet calloused, his face burned black just like a slave obeying Mozi's every command. Yet he never dared to give voice to his private desires. Under Mozi's ceaseless tutelage, many disciples of Mohism just like Qin Huali all grew step by step into worthy knights who could stimulate benefit and eradicate harm in the world for others.

The success of Mozi's educational program not only embodied the nurturing of talented knights, it also achieved a complete makeover for those who lacked talent or who had character flaws. The *Spring and Autumn Annals of Mr. Lü*, "Venerating Teachers" section records that once in the state of Qi there were two brutal men who caused much suffering among the people of their native region; one was named Gao He, and one was named Xian Zishi. There was nothing they would not do, and their crimes increased steadily. They later took refuge at the Mohist academy, and through Mozi's assiduous teaching and strict guidance, they ultimately became "famous knights and renowned personages" in the world.

In that age of radiant stars and a hundred voices competing to be heard, not only was Mozi himself a renowned figure esteemed by the world, his famous school for the common people and its teachings—Mohism—itself earned a wide reputation. Today after two thousand years, the educational thought of Mohism still maintains huge practical significance. It is just as Professor Wang Yu'an has stated, "The most prominent features of Mozi's educational program are its comprehensiveness and its practical training. Mozi's comprehensive education is embodied in the two aspects of the comprehensiveness of its educational thought and in the breadth of his educational content. Mozi emphasized practical experience in his educational program. The students whom he trained were able to learn practical

认为，学习不能仅仅停留在由感官获取的和从别人那里得来的直接知识，更重要的是能够对它们进行思辨、推论和求证，从而获得间接知识。他把这种认知的方法传授给学生，内化成学生自己的学习能力，从而达到更好的教学效果。正所谓"授人以鱼，不如授人以渔"，掌握了学习方法的墨家子弟和墨家后学们因此而不断发明、不断创新，将墨学推向了更高的巅峰。

在墨子以身作则的教化和伟大人格的感召下，墨家弟子都能为了行义"赴火蹈刃，死不还踵"。据《备梯》记载，禽滑厘跟随墨子三年，手和脚都起了老茧，脸也变得黧黑，像奴役一样听从墨子使唤，却从来不敢畅谈自己的私欲。在墨子不懈地教育下，许多和禽滑厘一样的墨家子弟都逐步成长为可以为天下兴利除害的贤士。

墨子教育的成功不仅体现在对有才之士的培养上，而且对那些缺乏才能或是品行有所欠缺的人，墨子也会想方设法使他们改头换面。《吕氏春秋·尊师》记载齐国曾有两个为乡里百姓痛恨的暴虐之人，一个叫高何，一个叫县子石。他们无恶不作，罪行累累。后来他们投奔到墨子门下，经过墨子的谆谆教诲和严格教导，最终也都成为"天下名士显人"。

在那个群星璀璨、百家争鸣的时代，不仅墨子自身为世人景仰，而他所创立的平民"显学"——墨家学说也是名扬天下。在两千多年后的今天，墨子的教育思想对我们仍有着巨大的现实意义。正如王裕安教授说："墨子的教育……其最突出的特点就是综合教育加实践锻炼。墨子的综合教育体现在教育思想的全面性和教育内容的广泛性两个方面。墨子在教育方法上注

knowledge; after completing their studies they were able to engage in the grand enterprise of saving society and aiding the people's livelihood, becoming the pillars of the state... Mozi's multi-disciplinarial education and emphasis on practical experience truly avoids certain defects in traditional education, and was a pioneering undertaking that was source of quality education." ❶

重实践，他所培养的学生能够学以致用，学成以后直接从事拯救社会和普济民生的大业，成为时代的栋梁之才。……墨子的多科教育和注重实践，实在是避传统教育之短，开素质教育之源的伟大创举。"❶

---

❶ 参见李广星：《墨学与当代教育》，中国书店出版社，1997年，第121—122页。

❶ See Li Guangxing, *Mozi and Contemporary Education*, China Bookstore Publishing House, 1997, pp. 121-122.

春秋耸肩尖足空首布——当时的一种货币
Raised Shoulder Sharp Feet Hollow Head Spade Coin
—A Kind of Currencies at that Time

十一　唯物师祖，精思巧辩

——墨家的"三表法"

Chapter XI　Founder of Materialism, Profound Thinker and Skilled Debater: The "Three Criteria" of Mohism

Mozi esteemed standards; he said, "Those who serve in the world cannot do without standards. There has never been a case where things are accomplished unless standards are used." ❶ In the actual course of production, he demanded that all the various tradesmen "make a square by means of a carpenter's square, make a circle by means of a compass, find a straight line by means of a line, make things level by means of water, correct things with a plum bob." ❷ But as for the discourse and perception of men, Mozi felt that it was also necessary to have a standard to follow. He said, "In judging whether discourse and perception are correct or not, it is necessary to have a unified standard for measuring. Otherwise it will be similar to trying to measure daylight in a revolving plate, impossible to calculate accurately."

In order to do this, Mozi proposed three standards for testing whether perceptions are true or false, calling them the "Three Criteria": "One is the foundation, one is the source, and one is the application. What is the foundation? Above, the foundation is in the affairs of the sage kings in ancient times. What is the source? Below it is in observing the realities as they appear to the eyes and ears of the common people. What is the application? Abolishing the use of punishments in government, and observing what is of benefit to the commoners and other people in the state." ❸

The first criterion, called "tracing the foundation," is the "affairs of the sage kings in ancient times." It is to use the historical acts of the sages, worthies, lords and kings as one standard to verify whether a perception is true or false. All perception, as long as it is commensurate with the actions of the ancient sage kings and verifies their experiences, affords a standard of correctness; if it is contrary to this, then it is erroneous. While refuting the fatalism of Confucianism, Mozi utilized the following standard: "In the past, Jie of Xia disturbed the world, and it required Tang to bring order. Zhou of Shang disturbed the world, and it required King Wu to bring order. The world did not change, neither did the people, so the monarch changed the laws, and the people then became easy to teach. In the same way, the people during the times of Tang of Shang and King Wu of Zhou became ordered. During the times of Jie of Xia and Zhou of Shang they became rebellious. Peril and order lay in the laws promulgated by the monarch, so how can one claim that it was due to fate?"

The second criterion, known as "tracing the origin," was "the realities of the eyes and ears of the common people." It used the direct experience gained through the eyes, ears and other sense organs of the people to serve as one of the standards for verifying the truth or falsity of perceptions. Whatever had

墨子崇尚法仪，他说："天下从事者，不可以无法仪。无法仪而其事能成者，无有。"❶在生产实践中，他要求百工"为方以矩，为圆以规，直以绳，衡以水，正以县。"❷而对于人的言论和认识，墨子认为也要有法可循。他说："判断言论和认识的正确与否，必须有一个统一的衡量标准，否则就会像在一个旋转着的盘子上测量日影一样，无法定准。"

为此，墨子提出了检验认识是非真假的三条标准，被称作"三表法"："有本之者，有原之者，有用之者。于何本之？上本之于古者圣王之事。于何原之？下原察百姓耳目之实。于何用之？废以为刑政，观其中国家百姓人民之利。"❸

第一表，所谓"本之者"，即"古者圣王之事"。将历史上的圣贤君王的事迹和经验作为检验认识是非真假的标准之一。一切认识，凡是吻合古代圣王的事迹和经验中存在的则为对，反之则为错。在批驳儒家命定论时，墨子便运用了这一标准："从前，夏桀搅乱了天下，由汤来治理；商纣搅乱了天下，由武王来治理。这个世界没有改变，人民也没有改变，君王改变了政令，人民就容易教导。同样的人民在商汤、周武王时就得到治理，在夏桀、商纣时则变得混乱。安危与治乱，在于君王发布的政令，怎么能说是有命呢！"

第二表，所谓"原之者"，即"百姓耳目之实"。将人们通过耳目等感官获取的直接经验作为检验认识是非真假的标准之

❶《法仪》。
❷《法仪》。
❸《非命上》。

❶ "Standards."
❷ "Standards."
❸ "Against Fatalism," Part One.

been heard or seen had existed; if not, it had not existed. It is evident that Mozi relied heavily on the perceptual experience of the people.

The third criterion, known as "abolishing the use of punishments in government, and observing what is of benefit to the commoners and other people in the state," indicates the application of understanding throughout all social experience, observing whether the effects of its practical utility are commensurate with the benefits of the state and the people. Here, although Mozi did not clearly indicate that practical experience was a standard for examining understanding, nevertheless his thinking emphasizing the benefits to the state and to the common people brilliantly manifested a totally fresh empathy for the people. His opposition to wars of aggression, opposition to extravagance and waste, opposition to predestination, etc., all take their points of departure from this.

In the history of Chinese philosophy, Mozi's "Three Criteria" rather early proposed the problem of a standard for examining the understanding of people. They used direct and indirect experience as the standard for examining whether understanding was correct or erroneous, at every point scattering glittering rays of simple materialism. Afterwards, whether Xunzi's "Tallying Experience," Han Feizi's "Comparative Verification," or Wang Chong's "Verifying Experience," all of them were deeply influenced by this. What cannot be denied is that the "Three Criteria" contain many inherent deficiencies. Mozi's epistemology is impossible to regard as an authentically scientific epistemology.

The major defect of the "Three Criteria" was in the one-sided and exaggerated role assigned to sense experience. Even more so did Mozi's epistemology remain stuck in indirect experience of people of the past and the direct experience obtained by the sense organs, and never did elevate perceptual understanding to the higher level of rational understanding, to the point where it was impossible to understand the essence of things. We all know that the sensory experience of man is not possible to be fully equivalent to objective truth. Under many conditions perceptions will be erroneous, illusory or false, containing many elements of probability. Yet Mozi regarded this as the standard for judging the correctness of understanding; the result of this was on the one hand denying the speciousness of the Mandate of Heaven theory, but on the other hand reaching the conclusion the ghosts existed based on the same arguments.

一。凡是听见过、看见过的就是存在的，反之就是不存在的。可见墨子对人的感性经验非常信赖。

第三表，所谓"废以为刑政，观其中国家百姓人民之利"，是指把认识贯彻于社会实践，看其实际应用的效果是否符合国家和人民的利益。在这里，墨子虽然没有明确提出以实践作为检验认识的标准，但其注重国家、百姓利益的思想却无不闪现着鲜明的人民性。他的反对侵略战争、反对铺张浪费、反对命定论等思想都是以此为出发点的。

墨子的"三表法"在中国哲学史上比较早地提出了检验认识的标准问题。他把人们的直接经验和间接经验作为检验认识是非对错的标准，处处闪烁着朴素唯物主义的光芒。此后，无论是荀子的"符验"、韩非子的"参验"，还是王充的"效验"，都深受其影响。不可否认的是，"三表法"的自身也存在有不少弊端，墨子的认识论还不能算作真正科学的认识论。

"三表法"的主要缺陷，就在于片面夸大了感觉经验的作用。墨子的认识论更多地停留在从前人那里得来的间接经验和从感觉器官获取的直接经验，而没有能把这些感性认识上升到理性认识的高度，以至于无法认识事物的本质。我们都知道，人的感觉经验并不能完全等同于客观真理，很多情况下会都出现错觉、幻觉和假象，带有很大的或然性。而墨子却以此作为判断认识对错的标准，这样做的结果是他一方面批驳着天命的虚无，另一方面却又根据同样的论证方法得出了鬼神存在的结论。

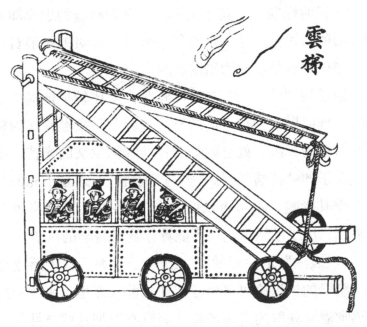

雲梯

中国古代用于攻城的"云梯"
Scaling Ladders for the Attack against Cities in Ancient China

十二　任人唯贤，倡导统一

——墨家的政治思想

Chapter XII　Meritocracy and the Advocacy of Unity: Mozi's Political Thought

"Elevating the Worthy" and "Identifying with One's Superior" are two important aspects of Mozi's political thought. Targeting the various defects in the system of appointment based on personal ties of the contemporary society, Mohists raised the glorious banner of the ancient worthies. He proposed "As for elevating the worthy, it is the basis of government," ❶ regarding selecting the worthy and employing the able as the decisive factor in managing a state in a fine manner.

Elevating the worthy, so-called, described in a more colloquial fashion is to respect, promote and employ worthy men. Utilizing men in government by those in power, always requires that being worthy or not is the standard for accepting or rejecting them. What kind of person is able to be called worthy? "Elevating the Worthy," Part Two, clearly demonstrates that a worthy person was a "knight who was worthy and fine, was replete in virtuous nature, discerning in words and speech, and broad in the techniques of the way." He not only had to possess superior moral qualities, but also needed to be good at words and speech and be erudite. Mohists felt that only such a "worthy and fine knight" who possessed this type of moral virtue and talent would be able to cause the state and great households to be enriched and strengthened, and the altars of soil and grain flourish. Nevertheless, rulers of the time usually "inevitably sought fine workmanship" in their clothing, "inevitably sought fine butchers" in slaughtering their oxen and sheep, "sought fine physicians" in healing their worn-out horses, and "inevitably sought fine workmen" in repairing their bows and arrows. ❷ In doing such daily commonplace work it was still necessary to seek out competent and skilled craftsmen; but in the great matter of ordering the state, it was not considered necessary to seek out the worthy; instead one's own relatives or handsome men were employed. Mohists revealed the absurdity of this kind of employment based on favoritism, and proposed the theory of elevating the worthy that employed men on the basis of meritocracy. Mohists also displayed to rulers the ideal results of having worthy men manage the state: Heaven and the spirits will grant wealth to you; the feudal princes will befriend you; the common people with attach themselves to you; worthy men will pledge allegiance to you. Your plans will certainly come to fruition; your affairs will certainly be successful; your defense of cities will be impregnable; you will crush all you face on expeditions.

Well, just how can one "elevate the worthy?" Mozi felt that, first of all, one must put into practice the following: "Do not be partisan towards one's own father and brothers; do not tend towards the noble or wealthy; do not dote on the handsome or attractive;" "do not distinguish between the poor and

　　"尚贤"和"尚同"是墨家政治思想的两个重要方面。针对当时社会任人唯亲所产生的种种弊病，墨家举起了古代尚贤的光辉旗帜，提出"夫尚贤者，政之本也"❶，把选贤任能看作治理好国家的决定性因素。

　　所谓尚贤，通俗地说就是尊重、提拔和任用贤人。执政者从政用人，都要以是否以贤能作为取舍标准。什么样的人才能称之为贤呢？《尚贤上》中明确表示，贤人就是"贤良之士"，是"厚乎德性，辩乎言谈，博乎道术"的人，不仅要有优良的品德，还要善于言谈、学识渊博。墨家认为，只有这样德才兼备的"贤良之士"才能使国家富强、社稷兴盛。然而当时的统治者平时做衣服"必索良工"，杀牛羊"必索良宰"，医疲马"必索良医"，修弓箭"必索良工"❷。做这些日常之事还知道要寻找能工巧匠，可在治理国家大事的时候却不知道寻求贤者，而是任用自己的亲人或者外表漂亮的人。墨家揭示了这种"任人唯亲"的荒谬性，提出"任人唯贤"的尚贤之说，并向统治者展示了贤人治国的理想结果：天鬼赐予你财富，诸侯与你结交，百姓与你亲附，贤人归顺于你。谋事定有所得，做事必会成功，守城固若金汤，出征所向披靡。

　　那么，怎样才能够"尚贤"呢？墨子认为，首先要做到"不党父兄，不偏贵富、不嬖颜色"，"不辩贫富贵贱、远迩亲

❶《尚贤上》。
❷《尚贤下》。
❶ "Elevating the Worthy," Part One.
❷ "Elevating the Worthy," Part Three.

wealthy and the noble and base, the near and far, distant relatives and close relatives; raise up the worthy and elevate them." ❶ This all means that, no matter whether the background of a person is wealthy or poor, his status noble or base, or whether his familial relationship is near or far, his appearance ugly or handsome, as long as he is virtuous and talented, then he should be employed with no hesitation. Mohists proclaimed with a loud voice, "No one should be venerated as noble in office on a permanent basis, and the people are not permanently base; those with ability should be elevated, and those lacking in ability should be demoted." ❷ This clearly demonstrates that elevating the worthy must break up the system of hereditary inheritance, and break up the limitations of social rank based on blood ties. At a time when society was based on the blood ties of the patriarchal clan system, this doubtlessly was a bold thing to advocate, possessing as it did revolutionary significance. Even up to the present day its glory still has not lost its dazzling nature.

As for how to employ the worthy after selecting them, Mozi cited a concrete example: If the state desired to gather more men who were good at archery and chariot driving, they must certainly enrich them, treat them nobly, and respect and praise them. Similar to this, as for worthies who rule the state, rulers must also "loftily endow them with rank, heavily endow them with emolument, employ them with assignments, and endow them with power to make decision." Only in this way will they be able to more effectively play their roles.

Before the Mohist school, Confucius also had previously proposed the similar advocacy of "illuminating the worthy," and also recommended employing the worthy to order the state. However, the nature of government by the worthy of Confucians was different than the nature of that advocated by Mohists. The scope of Confucian selection of the worthy was limited solely to upper class aristocrats, and could not allow "the base to surpass the noble, the distant to surpass the closely related." ❸ But Mozi rather stood on the side of the "peasants and craftsmen and merchants," clearly proposing to break up the system of hereditary aristocracy and to break through the limitations of the social rank and blood ties and let the worthy, noble as well as base, stand equal before all men. Mohists hoped to utilize a new type of standard for dividing social rank—being worthy and able to replace the old standard—the blood ties of the patriarchal clan system. This was an attack on government by the aristocracy of the time, and was a demand by the class of small producers to elevate their own social and political position, and to participate in the political hue and cry of managing the state. Nevertheless, given the blood ties of the

疏，贤者举而尚之"❶。也就是说，不管一个人的出身是穷还是富、身份是贵还是贱、和自己的关系是近还是远、长的是丑还是美，只要他有德有才，就要毫不犹豫地任用他。墨家大声呼告"官无常贵，而民无终贱，有能则举之，无能则下之"❷，明确提出举贤必须打破世袭制，打破尊卑血缘的局限。这在血缘宗法制社会的当时无疑是具有革命性的大胆主张，时至今日仍不减其耀眼的光辉。

关于选出贤者之后该如何任用，墨家举了一个具体的例子：如果国家想聚集更多的善于射箭和驾车的人，一定要使他们富裕、使他们尊贵，尊敬他们、赞誉他们。与之相同，对于治理国家的贤人，统治者也要"高予之爵，重予之禄，任之以事，断予之令"，这样才能使他们更好地发挥其作用。

在墨家之前，孔子也曾提出过类似的"明贤"主张。也提倡任用贤人以治理国家，不过儒家的贤人政治却与墨家有着本质的不同。儒家的选贤范围仅限于上层贵族，不可以"卑逾尊、疏逾戚"❸。而墨家却是站在"农与工肆之人"的立场上，明确提出打破贵族世袭制、打破尊卑血缘的局限、贤能面前人人平等。墨家希望以一种新的划分社会等级的标准——贤能，来代替旧的标准——宗法血缘。这是对当时贵族政治的抨击，是小生产者阶层要求提高自己的社会政治地位、参与国家管理的

❶《尚贤中》。
❷《尚贤上》。
❸《孟子·梁惠王下》。

❶ "Elevating the Worthy," Part Two.
❷ "Elevating the Worthy," Part One.
❸ Mencius, "King Hui of Liang," Part Two.

patriarchal clan system in the society of the time, it was hard to completely stamp it out; a government thoroughly run by worthy men was impossible to exist.

However, meritocracy as a kind of subjective ideal of the Mohists who represented the small producers rather represented the ideal of a kind of progressive society.

In addition to elevating the worthy, Mohists felt that "Identifying with One's Superior" was also a fundamental key to governing and for ordering the state. "Identifying with One's Superior" meant "unifying upwardly." Its basic content was to require that all thinking and conduct of men be unified at each class level from the bottom up. The commoners are unified with the officials, the lower level is united with the upper level, all-under-heaven is unified with the Son of Heaven, and lastly the Son of Heaven is unified with Heaven. The will of Heaven should be the highest standard for the speech and conduct of the people.

Mohists felt that before society produced administrative institutions, "one person had one view, two persons had two views, ten people had ten views." ❶ Each person felt that his "view" was correct, and the "view" of others was incorrect. Therefore they attacked each other, and injured each other, similar to a bunch of beasts and birds killing each other off. But society grows increasingly chaotic in this unceasing struggle. In order to change this type of chaotic condition where each has his own view, it was necessary to establish an effective administrative management system in order to unify the thought and conduct of the people. Therefore, Mohists proposed the theory of identifying upwardly to "unify the views of all-under-heaven," and sketched out stage by stage the blue print for an ideal political structure: first select a person of virtue and talent to be established as Son of Heaven, then select in order worthy and capable men to be established as Three Dukes, feudal lords, ministers, senior local officials or neighborhood leaders. Mohism demanded that each person who held an official post must be a worthy person; this was entirely in keeping with Mozi's thinking on "Elevating the Worthy."

If one states that the arrangement of this type of political structure was from top to bottom, in the course of actual administration it was from the bottom up; it started from the lowest level, and moved upward through each stage in a unified manner. Ultimately, through the Son of Heaven it was united with Heaven. For instance, the lowest level of neighborhood leader administered his own stewardship over his neighborhood according to the principles of the Son of Heaven; this unified the opinions within the neighborhood, and maintained a unity of opinion with the senior local official

政治呐喊。然而在当时的血缘宗法的社会关系下，任人唯亲是难以完全杜绝的，彻底的贤人政治也不可能存在。

不过，任人唯贤，作为小生产者代表的墨家的一种主观理想，它却代表了一种进步的社会理想。

除了尚贤，墨家认为"尚同"也是为政的根本和治理国家的关键。所谓"尚同"，即"上同"之义，其基本内涵是要求人们的一切思想、行动必须自下而上逐级统一。百姓统一于官员，下级统一于上级，天下统一于天子，天子最终统一于天。天的意志应该是人们言行的最高准则。

墨家认为，在社会还没有产生行政组织之前，"一人则一义，二人则二义，十人则十义"❶。每个人都认为自己的"义"是对的，别人的"义"是错的，因此就互相攻击、相互残害，就像一群自相残杀的禽兽，而社会就在这种不停的争斗中愈来愈乱。为了改变这种一人一义的混乱状态，必须建立行之有效的行政管理系统，以统一人们的思想和行动。因此，墨家提出"一同天下之义"的尚同之说，并一层一层勾勒出了理想中的政治结构蓝图：先选择德才兼备的人立为天子，再依次选择贤能之人立为三公、诸侯国君、卿大夫、乡长、里长。墨家要求担任各级官员的必须是贤人，这与他的"尚贤"思想也是一脉相承的。

如果说这种政治结构的设制是自上而下的话，那么在具体的施政过程中，则是自下而上，即由最下层开始，逐层向上统一，最终通过天子统一于上天。例如，最下层的里长根据天子

---

❶《尚同上》。

❶ "Identifying with One's Superior," Part One.

on the next level upward. The senior local official managed the stewardship of his own locality, unifying the opinions within his locality, and maintained a unity of opinion with the lord of the state on the next level upwardly. The lord of the state managed his own state, unifying the opinions within his state, and maintained a unity of opinion with the Son of Heaven on the next level upwardly. And what the Son of Heaven had to do was to maintain a unity with the Will of Heaven. In this manner the Will of Heaven was executed downward through successive stages. In the course of this process, "What is considered correct above, must be considered correct below; what is considered to be wrong above, must be considered wrong below." ❶Herein the opinion of the upper level was absolutely authoritative; lower levels must unconditionally obey it. Each person had to maintain a unity with the opinion of those on the upper levels, and could not collude together with those on a lower level. This is what Mohists meant by the phrase "identify upwardly and do not collude downwardly." Mohists felt that this type of political structure of identifying upwardly could facilitate the exchange of understanding between upper and lower levels, and hence make the governance and management of the state become more simple and effective. "Order the world like a state orders a family; treat the people in the world like a single person." ❷

What is worth noticing is that in the course of "unifying the opinions in the world," Mohists only mentioned "selecting the most worthy in the world and establish him as the Son of Heaven." ❸ That is, they did not specifically indicate who it was that would "select the most worthy in the world." This means that a problem was created when Mohists did not state who would select the Son of Heaven who clearly was the most senior administrative official. Because this phrase lacked a grammatical subject, some scholars feel that the selection of the Son of Heaven should be made by the people, and some scholars feel that the Heaven above would select the Son of Heaven. Actually, in the thought of Mohism, Heaven above represented the interests of the people. Therefore, regardless of who the grammatical subject was, the ultimate goal of identifying upwardly was to work unitedly for the interests of the people.

Granted that this type of idealism of identifying upwardly was a beautiful thing, nevertheless because Mohists persistently stressed the obedience of the lower levels towards the upper ones, they ignored the restraints placed on the upper levels by the lower levels. This then was bound to result in unrestricted expansion of the authority of the Son of Heaven, and ultimately led to an extreme form of dictatorship. Although Mohists selected Heaven to control the Son of Heaven, an illusory Heaven above had no effectual binding force to

的原则治理自己管辖的里，使里内意见一致，并与上一层的乡长保持意见一致；乡长治理自己管辖的乡，使乡内意见一致，并与上一层的国君保持意见一致；国君治理自己的国家，使国内意见一致，并与上一层的天子保持意见一致。而天子要做的是与天的意志保持一致，天的意志就这样一层层地落实下来。在这过程中，"上之所是必亦是之，上之所非必亦非之" ❶。在这里，上级的意见有着绝对的权威性，下级必须无条件服从。人人都要与上级的意见保持一致，而不能与下级朋比为奸，这就是墨家所说的"上同而不下比"。墨家认为，这种尚同的政治结构可以使上下通情，从而使国家的统治和管理变得简便而有效："治天下之国若治一家，使天下之民若使一夫" ❷。

值得注意的是，在"一同天下之义"的过程中，墨家只说"选天下之贤可者，立以为天子" ❸，却并没有特别指出是谁来"选天下之贤可者"。也就是说墨家并没有明确作为最高行政长官的天子是由谁来推选产生的问题。由于缺少主语，有学者认为应当是由人民选择天子，也有学者认为是上天选择天子。其实在墨家的思想中，上天代表的就是人民的利益。因此，无论这里的主语是谁，尚同的终极目标都是统一于人民的利益。

这样的尚同理想固然是美好的，然而，由于墨家一味地强调下级对上级的服从，却忽略了下级对上级的制约，这就势必带来天子权利的无限扩大，最终导致极端的独裁主义。墨家虽

❶《尚同中》。
❷《尚同下》。
❸《尚同上》。

❶ "Identifying with One's Superior," Part Two.
❷ "Identifying with One's Superior," Part Three.
❸ "Identifying with One's Superior," Part One.

restrain the Son of Heaven. Therefore, even though the original intention of the Mohists perhaps was not so conceived, their theory of upward identification instead stressed the centralized rule of the sovereign. During the era of wars among the feudal states and chaotic societies of the Spring and Autumn and Warring States Periods, this actually conformed to the trend of historical development of the times. Later on, as absorbed and expanded by the Legalists, the theory of identifying upwardly evolved into the intellectual foundation for centralized rule on the part of monarchs, establishing the basis for the fundamental pattern of two thousand years of feudal government.

然搬出"天"来管制天子，但虚无缥缈的上天实际对天子并没有任何有效的约束力。因此，尽管墨家的本意或许并非如此，但是他的尚同学说却强调了君主的集权统治。这在诸侯征战、社会混乱的春秋战国之际，是符合当时历史发展趋势的。后来经由法家的吸收和发扬，尚同学说进而演变成为君主集权统治的思想基础，奠定了中国两千年封建政治的基本格局。

孙诒让像和《墨子闲诂》书影

Portrait of Sun Yirang and Picture of *Annotations on Mozi*

十三 由盛而衰，否极泰来

——墨学的衰亡与复兴

Chapter XIII From Apogee to Decline, after Misfortune Comes Good Fortune: The Decline and Renaissance of Mohism

Much investigation and analysis, both anciently and in modern times, has gone into the reasons for the decline and disappearance of Mohism. Zhuangzi concluded that Mohist advocacy of hard work for the living and shabby funerals for the dead ran counter to general human nature, making it hard to be accepted. Ban Gu on the other hand felt that the reason for the decline and disappearance of the Mohist school was due to its theories that kept the people ignorant of the rites, and did not distinguish between near and far relationships.

In recent times, scholarly circles have conducted many inquiries into this question. In the thirties of the twentieth century, Fang Shouchu summarized the views of such scholars as Hu Shi, Liang Qichao, Li Ji and Guo Moruo in his work *The Origins of Mohism*: First was because of the opposition of Confucians; second was because of the jealousy of politicians; third was the sophistry of later Mohists being too abstruse; fourth was that the failure of the class uprising led by Chen She and Wu Guang made it impossible for Mohism to survive since it was associated with the aims of the uprising in benefiting the people. Fifth was that it failed because it ran counter to social development.❶

The great and profound system of culture and thought that was Mohism ran through its own course of creation, development and transformation. The political, economic and intellectual culture of Chinese society was varied in its nature and regulations. Therefore, viewing a single subjective or objective aspect to investigate the reason for the decline and disappearance of Mohism is one-sided and cannot stand. We feel that its decline and disappearance was not only due to the fatal defects inherent in its doctrine, but externally it lacked a social environment conducive to its growth towards the next stage.

In the preface to his *Annotations on Mozi*, Yu Yue said, "Mozi was able to identify with superiors because of universal love, he was able to oppose offensive warfare because he identified with superiors, he was able to be particular about methods of defensive warfare because of his opposition to offensive warfare." "Universal Love" was the core of Mohist thought; on this foundation Mohists inferred a political system centered on "ten theories." To a certain degree, Mohist theory is nothing other than the theory of "Universal Love". Therefore, the decline and disappearance of Mohism cannot be separated from its close relationship with the thought of "Universal Love."

Mozi advocated universal love, and criticized the Confucian standpoint on "the art of cherishing relatives, and venerating the worthy according to their station." ❷ He demanded that "one regards other's states as your own state, regard other's family as your own family, regard another's person as you

关于墨学衰亡的原因，古往今来，人们进行过许多探索和分析。庄子认为，墨家主张活着的人要勤劳，死去的人要薄葬，这样的学说违背了一般的人性，很难使人接受。班固则认为墨家衰亡是因为墨家学说使人不知礼仪，不别亲疏。

近代以来，学界对这一问题亦多有探讨。二十世纪三十年代方授楚在《墨学源流》一书中，归纳了胡适、梁启超、李季、郭沫若等人的看法：一是由于儒家的反对；二是由于墨家学说遭政客猜忌；三是由于墨家后学的"诡辩"太微妙了；四是因陈涉、吴广领导的阶级革命的失败使代表其利益的墨学无法幸存；五是墨学逆社会发展而失败。❶

墨学这个博大精深的文化思想体系，有其产生、发展和演变的过程。中国社会的政治、经济和思想文化亦具有多种多样的性质和规定。因此，单从主观或客观某一方面来探讨墨学衰亡的原因都是片面而不可取的。我们认为，墨学的衰亡不仅在自身学理上存在有致命缺陷，而且在外部也没有使其进一步成长的社会环境。

俞樾在《墨子间诂》序文中说："墨子惟兼爱是以尚同，惟尚同是以非攻，惟非攻是以讲求备御之法。""兼爱"是墨家思想的核心，在此基础上墨家推演出了以"十论"为主要内容的政治思想体系。从某种意义上讲，墨家的学说就是"兼爱"的学说。因此，墨家的衰亡与"兼爱"思想有着密不可分的关系。

墨子倡导兼爱，批评儒家"亲亲有术，尊贤有等"❷的观点，要求"视人之国若视其国，视人之家若视其家，视人之身

❶ 方授楚：《墨学源流》，中华书局，1989，第202—205页。
❷ 《非儒下》。

❶ Fang Shouchu, *The Origins of Mohism*, Zhonghua Book Co., 1989, pp.202-205.
❷ "Against the Confucians," Part Two.

regard your own person." ❶ This is to say, one should not separate people into classes or ranks; no matter what a person's status or position is, they should love each other universally and equally. Granted, this reflected the simple aspirations of the lower middle class of laborers of the time, nevertheless on the foundation of a feudal society based on the system of patriarchal hierarchy, as a national policy universally undertaken, it can only be regarded as impractical wishful thinking.

Regardless whether we are talking about the slave age or the feudal age, the Chinese people never cast off the blood relationships of the clan system. Self-sufficient small farmers naturally formed modes of production based on the family units, making the clan system based on the linkages of blood-tie relationships extend through time and be retained over the ages. During the Spring and Autumn and Warring States Periods, although some "peasants, craftsmen and merchants" shrugged off the shackles of the patriarchal system of family communes, exerting enormous pressure on the patriarchal system, nevertheless the patriarchal system was not shaken from its position as the foundation of ancient Chinese society. The patriarchal ideal that was deeply etched on the hearts of the people early on took deep root, forming a firm ethnic mentality, social mentality and ethical framework.

As far as the ruling class went, only through establishing the position of cherishing one's family relationships within the patriarchal system was it possible to evolve venerating those senior to oneself, and establish on this foundation a political system and political order, and from this fix their supreme political authority. As far as the commoners went, they were required to love each other as themselves, and share whatever wealth they possessed with others, making them destroy their own clan systems, and destroy the disparities of poverty and wealth, and ranks of noble and base. This kind of treatment was completely antithetical to the disparity among relationships under the patriarchal clan system, and was also completely antithetical to the system of private ownership of class society. It was exactly like one scholar has said, "Speaking of Mozi's universal love, in all actuality, as long as family blood ties exist in the human race and as long as private ownership and private ideals exist, as long as the recognition of self and others exists, the so-called ideals of loving one's father like one own's father and harming oneself to benefit others will never be able to form a universal ideology and system of conduct. This is to say that what Mozi advocated lacked a real foundation for it to exist, and can only be described as a kind of fantasy. Therefore, it is no wonder that within the history of the development of ancient Chinese thought,

若视其身。" ❶ 就是说人与人之间不分阶级、阶层，无论身份、地位，都要普遍地、平等地相爱，这固然反映了当时中下层劳动人民的朴素愿望，然而要在以宗法等级制为基础的封建社会里作为一种国策来普遍推行，只能成为不切实际的一厢情愿。

无论是奴隶时代还是封建时期，中国人都没有摆脱氏族血缘关系。自给自足的小农自然经济形成了以家族为单位的生产方式，使以血缘关系为纽带的宗法制度得以延续下来并长期保留。春秋战国时期，虽然一部分 "农与工肆之人" 摆脱了家长制家庭公社的羁绊，给宗法制带来巨大冲击，但宗法制在中国古代社会的基石地位并没有被动摇。深深烙在人们心底的宗法观念早已根深蒂固，成为牢固的民族心态、社会心态与伦理规范。

对于统治阶级而言，只有奠定宗法关系中的亲亲本位，才能衍化出尊尊，并以此建立政治体制和政治秩序，从而确定他们至高无上的统治权力。对于一般百姓来说，要他们爱人如爱己、有了钱财要分给别人，让他们去打破家族本位，打破人与人之间原有的贫富、贵贱的地位。这种做法与宗法制下的亲疏差别水火不容，也与阶级社会的私有制度背道而驰。正如有学者所说："就墨子的兼爱来说，事实上只要人类的家庭血缘关系存在，只要私有制和私有观念还存在，只要人与我的意识还存在，所谓爱人之父如爱己之父和专门亏己以利人，就绝不可能成为一种普遍的意识和行为。也就是说，墨子的主张没有真实的存在基础，只能说是一种空想。所以，无怪乎在中国古代思想发展史上墨家学说中绝，后世的人们都不再提倡和实践其

---

❶ 《兼爱中》。

❶ "Universal Love," Part Two.

Mohism disappeared, and men of later generations no longer advocated or carried out what it taught." ❶ Mencius criticized Mozi's "Universal Love" as "lacking a father," as "being like the birds and beasts." ❷ Although this wording was somewhat excessive, it nevertheless grasped the incompatibility of the theory of "Universal Love" with the nature of the patriarchal clan system, dealing a death blow to Mohist theory that led to its demise.

Fundamentally speaking, the theory of "Universal Love" contains too much coloration of phantasy, and was not appropriate for the demands of developing contemporary social production forces. While still far distant from being able to develop production forces to the point of implementing "Universal Love," Mozi was too far ahead of his times in promoting this, and forcedly demanded change in the relationship between production forces and the superstructure that was not appropriate for the development of production forces of the time. In this way his theories that soared above history were like water without a source, like a tree without roots, and only able to function as castles in the sky to provide spiritual comfort for people in an age of disorder, unable to possess permanent vitality. Attempting to implement love that transcended class in a class-based society was a universal love that was impractical; its appearance at the birth of Mohism sealed the tragic destiny of Mohism's decline and disappearance.

Opposite to this was the humaneness and love sought by Confucians that was built on the hierarchical love founded on cherishing human relationships. This type of love based on the blood ties of the patriarchal clan system was adapted to the needs of the development of production forces, and also complied with actual social conditions of the time and the demands of the rulers. Therefore, following the arrival of the age of grand unification and solidification of feudal rule, it became a historical necessity that Confucianism would rise and Mohism would decline. It was precisely as Mr. Qian Mu said, "Although Confucius did not mention the supreme god and did not approach religion, still he did have chapels. The family and ancestral temple were the chapels of Confucius. Although Mozi did not advocate the supreme god, and also closely approached religion, nevertheless he did not have a chapel, because he did not respect the family and ancestral temples. Mozi ultimately did not grasp human nature; Mozi's theories lacked a profound and stable foundation, and also contravened the traditional spirit of the ancient Chinese which evolved from clan sentiment to the humanistic viewpoint. Therefore, in the future Mohist thought was swallowed up by Confucian thought, and was unable to circulate." ❸

主张。" ❶孟子批评墨子"兼爱"是"无父",是"禽兽" ❷,虽然言辞过于激烈,却也抓住了"兼爱"学说不合宗法制的实质,击中了墨学骤衰的要害。

从根本上讲,"兼爱"学说空想色彩太过浓厚,不适合当时社会生产力的发展要求。在生产力还远远没有发展到推行"兼爱"的程度的时候,墨子却过于超前地将之提出,强行要求改变适合当时生产力发展的生产关系与上层建筑。这样凌驾于历史之上的学说是无源之水、无本之木,只能成为在乱世给人们一时心灵寄托的空中楼阁,不可能具有长久的生命力。企图在阶级的社会里推行超阶级的爱,这种不切实际的兼爱思想在诞生之初便就注定了墨家衰亡的悲剧命运。

与之相反,儒家讲求的仁爱是建立在亲亲基础之上的有差等的爱。这种以宗法血缘关系为根基的爱,适应了当时生产力发展的需要,也符合当时的社会实际和统治者的需求。所以,随着大一统时代的来临和封建统治的巩固,儒兴而墨绝就成为历史的必然。正如钱穆先生所说:"孔子虽然不讲上帝,不近宗教,但孔子却有一个教堂。家庭和宗庙,便是孔子的教堂。墨子虽主张有上帝,迹近宗教,但墨子缺乏一个教堂,因他不看重家庭与宗庙。墨子到底把捉不到人心,墨子的学说便缺乏深稳的基础,又违反了中国古代由家族情感过渡到人道观念的传统精神。因此在将来,墨家思想便为儒家思想所掩盖,不能畅行。" ❸

---

❶ 梁韦弦、李春生:《孟子与杨墨两家的论争》,《河北师范大学学报》(哲学社会科学版)
  1994年第1期。
❷ 《孟子·滕文公下》。
❸ 钱穆:《中国文化史导论》,商务印书馆,1994年,第84页。

❶ Liang Weixian and Li Chunsheng, "Mencius and his dispute with Yangzi and Mozi," *Journal of the Hebei Normal University (Philosophy and Social Science Edition)*, 1994, Issue 1.
❷ *Mencius*, "Duke of Tengwen," Part Two.
❸ Qian Mu, *Introductory Remarks on Chinese Cultural History*, The Commercial Press, 1994, p. 84.

Among pre-Qin philosophers, Mozi was the earliest to recognize that humanity depended on production through hard work, and that where humanity differed from other animals was in the notion that "those who relied on labor survived, while those who did not labor did not survive." ❶ Because he profoundly recognized the difficulty and importance of production, Mozi strenuously advocated "frugality in consumption" and "frugal burials," insisted that "if increased costs do not increase benefits to the people, then desist," and opposed any form of "useless expenditures." He indicated that dwellings required no carved beams or painted ridgepoles, all that was necessary was to provide shelter from the wind and rain. Clothing did not need to be extravagant, it just needed to fit the body. After a death there was no need for a luxurious burial and the wasting of the resources of society, and no need for three years mourning of relatives and the ruination of social production. From all of this he took an additional step in promoting the thought of "Against Music," feeling that music "violently seized the property of the people in the form of clothing and food," ❷ and that "the more music multiplies, the less orderly government grows."

Regardless of whether the age is the pre-Qin period of more than two thousand years ago or today during the twenty-first century, the frugality advocated by Mohist has an enormous practical value. Nevertheless, to go too far is as bad as not going far enough. The following examples doubtlessly limited the ultimate in eternal human ideal to the most basic needs of shelter and food, thus contravening the objective laws of social economic development: limiting consumption to barely enough to supply the basic needs of the protection of clothing and warding off of hunger by food; only seeking protection in housing from the wind and rain, cold and heat; avoiding rituals that separate male from female; seeking only "sturdiness in boats and speed in chariots;" and seeking only burial cloths that are "sufficient for rotten flesh" and coffins that are sufficient for "rotten corpses." And "Against Music" completely negated pursuits at the level of the human spirit. Maslow felt that the most primitive and fundamental physiological human needs are food, clothing, shelter, medicine, etc. In addition to these needs, humanity further requires the needs of safety, social interaction, respect and self-actualization. High-level needs have a greater value than low-level needs, and approach closest to human nature. Mozi's theory of "Against Music" overly stressed human physiological needs, and neglected other human needs at the higher level.

Actually, as early as the time of Zhuangzi, this great defect of Mohism

在先秦诸子中，墨子最早看到人类的生存要靠努力生产，而人类异于其他动物的地方也在于人类是"赖其力者生，不赖其力者不生" ❶。由于深刻认识到生产的不易性与重要性，墨子在消费方面力主"节用"、"节葬"，坚持"加费不加民利则止"，反对任何形式的"无用之费"。他提出住房不要雕梁画栋、能避风雨即可；穿衣不要讲求奢华、能合乎身体即可；人死了不要厚葬而浪费社会资财，亲人不要守丧三年而贻误社会生产。并由此进一步提出"非乐"思想，认为礼乐是"暴夺民衣食之财" ❷，"其乐逾繁者，其治逾寡"。

无论是在两千多年前的先秦时期还是在21世纪的今天，墨家倡导的节俭都有极强的现实价值。然而过犹不及，将消费限制到衣食只求饱暖，住房只求避风寒湿热、"别男女之礼"，舟车只求"完固轻利"，葬礼只求葬衣"足以朽肉"、棺木"足以朽骸"的层次，无疑是将人生的终极理想永远定格在了低层次的饱暖需求上，这违反了人类社会经济发展的客观规律。而"非乐"则更是完全否定了人类精神层次的追求。马斯洛认为：吃饭、穿衣、住宅、医疗等是人们最原始、最基本的生理需要。除了这些需要，人类还依次拥有安全需要、社交需要、尊重需要和自我实现需要。高层次的需要比低层次的需要有更大的价值，更接近于人类的天性。墨子的"非乐"理论过分强调了人的生理需要，却忽视了人的需要的其他更高层次。

其实早在庄子之时，就已看清了墨学的这一巨大缺憾。在

---

❶《非乐上》。
❷《辞过》。

❶ "Against Music," Part One.
❷ "Rejecting Excesses."

was already recognized. In *Zhuangzi*, "The World," Zhuangzi was the first to praise the noble sentiments of Mozi's "teaching later ages to avoid extravagance, frugality in the use of things, prevention of glaring differences in classes, pride in the use of the carpenter's line marker, and urgency to aid the world." Continuing on, he also clearly pointed out that Mozi's deficiencies lay in his practices of "no song in life, no burial clothing in death, a simple coffin with no outer one" that were excessively harsh to the extent of "teaching this to the people unfortunately would not be loving the people; putting this into practice would certainly not be loving oneself." Therefore, although Mozi preached "in life be diligent, in death be frugal," nevertheless because "his Way was greatly dreadful," and "he made others worried, he made them sad, and his method was hard to implement; I am afraid his Way was not that of the sages." The ultimate conclusion is that what Mozi's theory advocated was "contrary to the mind of the world, and the world could not endure it. Although he was able to practice it himself, how could the world do so? Being thus distanced from the world, he was far from being a king!" Obviously, Zhuangzi felt that being "contrary to the mind of the world, and the world could not endure it" was the fundamental reason that led to the rapid decline of Mohism.

Mohists overly stressed the benefits that they were able to achieve, and neglected to emphasize formal aesthetics within the spirit of Chinese humanism. In the face of the tradition of music and rites that were formed since the Xia, Shang and Zhou dynasties, the Mohists could only doggedly simplify and negate. They did not realize the need to develop along with material culture, that the development and evolution of the spiritual world also exists, and the pursuit of human aesthetics is a separate reality. Therefore, Liang Qichao said, "The most important reason for the failure of Mohism was its insistence on a life of duty without having a life of enjoyment as well." ❶

In addition to huge defects in its theory, the existential form of the Mohist school was another important reason for its extinction. Different than other pre-Qin intellectual schools, the existential form of the Mohist school possessed a tight method of management and standardized organizational format, and exhibited a fresh governmental purpose and urgent desire to expand. They were already different from the general run-of-the-mill scholarly organizations, and resembled more closely a half militarized conglomeration with a religious nature. This type of close organizational format, in its earliest formation, truly was more attention-grabbing than general scholarly organizations, and quickly effected a broad influence throughout society. Nevertheless, when any theory relies on how the sponsoring institution

《庄子·天下》中，庄子首先对墨子"不侈于后世，不靡于万物，不晖于数度，以绳墨自矫而备世之急"的高尚情操大加赞赏。接着又明确指出墨子的不足之处在于其"生不歌，死不服，桐棺三寸而无椁"的做法过于苛刻，以至"以此教人，恐不爱人;以此自行，固不爱己。"所以，虽然墨子"其生也勤，其死也薄"，却由于"其道大觳"而"使人忧，使人悲，其行难为也，恐其不可以为圣人之道"。最后得出结论: 墨子这样的学说主张"反天下之心，天下不堪。墨子虽能独任，奈天下何! 离于天下，其去王也远矣!"显然，庄子认为"反天下之心，天下不堪"是导致墨学迅速衰微的根本原因。

墨家过于强调能够实现的利益，却忽视了中国人文精神中对形式美的重视。面对夏商周以来形成的礼乐传统，墨家只是一味地简化和否定。他们不知道，与物质文明发展相伴的，还有着精神世界的发展和进化，还有着人类对美的追求。所以梁启超说:"弄到只有义务生活，没有趣味生活，墨学失败最重要的原因，就在于此。"❶

除了学理上的巨大缺陷，墨家学派的存在形式也是致其湮灭的重要原因。与先秦其他学术派别不同，墨家有着严密的管理方法和规范的组织形式，表现出鲜明的政治意图和迫切的发展欲望。他们已经不同于一般的学术团体，而更像是一个具有宗教性质的半军事化集团。这种严密的组织形式在产生之初，确实比一般的学术团体更加引人注目，可以迅速在社会上产生

❶ 蔡尚思:《十家论墨》，上海人民出版社，2004 年，第16页。

❶ Cai Shangsi, *Ten Specialists on Mozi*, Shanghai People's Publishing House, 2004, p. 16.

is organized, the length of existence of the organization then determines the length of the fate of the theory.

After Mozi died, the Mohist school never produced any leader who enjoyed such an exalted reputation or possessed such an ability to bring people together. After the heroic deaths of Meng Sheng and over 180 Mohist followers whom he had led to defend the lord of Yangcheng, the originally tightly organized Mohist institution unavoidably split apart, and step by step advanced toward its destination of decline and disappearance. This doubtlessly was a fatal blow to the Mohist doctrine that depended on organization for its existence. It was precisely as Fang Shouchu described it, "Mohism was a tightly organized institution; as soon as it split up, it suffered great injury." ❶In addition, Mohists possessed a real military force that cannot be slighted, internally, it also possessed law and discipline that outsiders could not learn about. This was something an autocratic administration could not countenance. After the Qin Dynasty unified the empire, this half-militarized organization that was both civil and military changed into an alien force posed against the ruling class. This class absolutely could not countenance this type of organization standing outside the limits of its own rule. Therefore, the Mohist organization became the target of oppression and destruction of the rulers under the Qin and Han, and Mohist theories also followed the disappearance of the organization and naturally became eliminated.

In addition to its own intrinsic reasons, such external changes as great transformations in the social environment and the disappearance of its class foundation were factors that cannot be overlooked. The class formed by small producers once had been active for a time during the Warring States Period; they yearned for peace and stability, opposed exploitation and oppression, and had their own interests at heart. Under this type of historical situation, Mohists who stressed compulsory military service became the spokespersons for these "peasants, craftsmen and merchants" and painted a picture of an ideal state, providing a wonderful source of spiritual support; therefore their followers became numerous.

In addition to this, the historical environment in which a hundred schools vied for attention was another external reason for Mohism becoming a renowned school. The Warring States Period was a unique age in which intellectuals became independent personalities. In order to stand firm in an age of fierce wars of annexation and to develop themselves, each feudal lord vied with each other to recruit scholars and to support them, and so any type of scholarly theory and current could be found within the intellectual fervor of the

广泛影响。然而任何学说一旦依附于组织，组织存在时间的长短也就决定了学说命运的长短。

墨子死后，墨家再没有出现过像他一样拥有崇高威望和巨大凝聚力的领袖人物。在孟胜率领一百八十余位墨家子弟为阳城君殉死之后，原本组织严密的墨家团体不可避免地走上了分裂之路，一步步地走向了衰亡的终点。这对于依附组织生存的墨家学说来讲无疑是一个致命的打击。正如方授楚所说："墨家为一有严密组织之团体，一经分裂，其害甚大。"❶再加上墨家拥有的不可小觑的军事实力，其团体内部还有着外人无法染指的法纪，这些都是专制政府所不能容忍的。在秦统一天下之后，这个文武兼备的半军事化集团就变成了统治阶级的异化力量，他们绝不会允许这样的组织凌驾于自己的统治之外。于是，墨家团体就成为秦汉统治者镇压消灭的对象，墨家学说也随着组织的消失而自然消亡。

除了墨学自身的原因，社会环境的巨大转变、阶级基础的不复存在等外部变化也是墨学衰微不可忽视的因素。由小生产者组成的阶层在春秋战国时期曾经活跃一时，他们向往和平安定，反对剥削压迫，有着自身的利益要求。在这种历史条件下，讲求役夫之道的墨家以这一阶级代言人的身份为这些"农与工肆之人"描绘了一个理想国，给他们提供了一个美好的心灵依托，因而信徒众多。

除此之外，百家争鸣的历史环境条件，也是墨家成为显学的外部原因之一。春秋战国时期是中国古代少有的知识分子人格独立的时代。为了在激烈的兼并战争中站稳脚跟并取得发展，各诸侯国都争相取士、养士，任何学说和思想都可以存在和争

---

❶ 方授楚：《墨学源流》，中华书局，1989，第207页。

❶ Fang Shouchu, *The Origins of Mohism*, Zhonghua Book Co., 1989, p. 207.

time vying for attention. Although Mohism was never officially implemented in any state, this did not prevent it from spreading throughout each state and quickly becoming a renowned school.

Nevertheless, Qin conquered all in the four directions, unified the empire, and China commenced the more than two thousand years of its feudal age. The small producer class represented by Mohism started to become integrated within the economic and political networks of feudalism, gradually becoming accepted within the bounds of the feudal patriarchal system. It evolved into a small producer under the feudal system, losing the historical position of its own independent existence. As the spokespersons of this class, Mohism also lost the soil and climate that provided its development, and thus was unable to remain independent and stay in existence. Mohism was thereby forced to withdraw from the stage of history.

However, Mohism was never without the possibility of making a recovery or lacking a time when it would once again emerge. After two thousand years of long waiting, following the intellectual enlightenment at the juncture of the Ming and Qing dynasties, the door of its restoration slowly opened up.

During the last years of the Ming Dynasty, intellectual thought became more and more active. Some intellectuals started to break through the restrictions of Confucianism, and outside of the sphere of traditional Confucianism explored new intellectual territory; this established the first philosophical foundation for the restoration of Mohism. By the Qianlong and Jiaqing eras of the mid Qing, research into Mohism also gradually reappeared following the flourishing of evidential research and research into the various ancient philosophical masters. Scholars started collecting materials, editing scattered remains of ancient Mohist manuscripts, and Mohism became a popular topic of research in academic circles of the time.

The one who was the source for Mohism research was the thinker Wang Zhong. He annotated *Mozi*, and collected materials within other ancient works on Mozi and edited *Indicating Subtleties in Mozi*. In an age when Confucianism enjoyed exclusive veneration and regarded Mohism as a "heretical doctrine," he boldly promoted a new understanding much different from the tradition, considering that Mozi was a humane and talented scholar who worked actively to save the world. He did his utmost to restore Mozi's fame. Even when branded with the reputation of "Mohist Wang Zhong," he did not knuckle under. Ever since that time, the value of Mohism gradually became recognized, even some orthodox Confucian scholars also joined the ranks of editing and researching *Mozi*. Some of these were renowned scholars, such as

鸣。墨学虽从未在任何一个国家真正实施过，但这并不妨害它在各国传播并迅速成为显学。

然而，秦毕四海，一统天下，中国开始了两千多年的封建时代。墨学所代表的小生产者阶层开始融入封建的经济政治关系之中，逐渐被纳入封建宗法制度的藩篱，演变为封建制度下的小生产者，失去了自己独立存在的历史地位。作为这一阶层的代言人，墨学也就失去了供其发展的土壤和气候，也就不可能独立的出现和存在下去了。

墨学就这样无奈地退出了历史舞台。不过墨学并没有从此一蹶不振，再无出头之日。经过两千年的漫长等待之后，随着明清之际的思想启蒙运动，复兴之门终于缓缓敞开。

明代末期，学术思想越来越活跃，一部分知识分子开始突破儒学的禁锢，在传统儒学范围之外探索新的知识领域，为墨学复兴奠定了最初的思想基础。到了清中叶乾嘉时期，随着考据学、诸子学研究的兴盛，墨学研究也逐渐复苏。人们开始收集、整理残存下来的《墨子》古籍，墨学成为当时学界研究的热点。

首开墨学研究之源的是思想家汪中。他曾为《墨子》作过校注，并收集古籍中涉及墨子的材料编成《墨子表微》。在儒学独尊、墨学被视为"异端"的当时，他大胆地提出了与传统不同的新见解，认为墨子是积极救世的仁人才士。他极力为墨子正名，即使被扣上"墨者汪中"的帽子也毫不屈服，为墨学的复兴营造出最初的舆论。从此，墨学的价值逐渐被人们重新认识，甚至连一些儒家正统学者也加入到整理、研究《墨子》的行列。他们之中不乏一些著名的学者，如：卢文弨、毕沅、王念孙、孙星衍、张惠言、王引之、俞樾、孙诒让等。其中又

Lu Wenchao, Bi Yuan, Wang Niansun, Sun Xingyan, Zhang Huiyan, Wang Yinzhi, Yu Yue, Sun Yirang, et al. Among them, the most influential research results were made by Bi Yuan and Sun Yirang.

Bi Yuan was the first one to synthesize the research of others and to make a systematic commentary on *Mozi*. In the *Preface to a Commentary on Mozi* which he composed, he fully confirmed the value of Mohism, considering that Mozi's theories "comprehended the authority of the classics; this point is incontestable." ❶ Even more so, Sun Yirang spent ten years of effort to compile the pinnacle of scholarship on Mozi of the time, his *Annotations on Mozi*. The great ancient text scholar of the Qing Dynasty, Yu Yue, praised this work as "nothing like it has appeared since the time of Mozi." ❷

Through the research and dissemination of these scholars, Mohism which had remained silent for two thousand years saw the first rays of light of its restoration. After the Opium War, with the deepening of the crises of the Chinese people following the unceasing invasion of Western culture, when some scholars were pleasantly surprised to discover in Mozi some similarities with western science, they could not wait to raise the banner of Mohism to strike back at the challenge of "gradual penetration of Western learning in the East." They considered Mohism to be on the exact level as Western science, even desiring to use this to resist the dissemination of Western learning. Among them was Zou Boqi, who led out in advocating the theory of "Western learning being of Chinese origin," who felt that Western astronomy, calendar, mathematics, etc. were all included within the scope of the *Mozi*. And Wang Kaiyun considered that the *Mozi* was the source of Western religions; Xue Fucheng also felt that the source of the Christianity of the West was to be found in the *Mozi*. Huang Zunxian even verified from five different angles that Western learning was traceable to Mohism, concluding that "up to the present day, each nation around the globe enacts the way of Mozi, seven parts out of ten." ❸ From science and religion to politics and ethics, *Mozi* of the times almost became an all-embracing encyclopedia for Western learning. Various types of far-fetched theories all demonstrated defects and use of research into Mohism of the time.

After the Sino-Japanese war of 1894-1895, whether we are speaking of the reformist school or revolutionary school, both of them profoundly realized that in order to save the Chinese people who were tottering on the edge of destruction, it was necessary to first recast the great national spirit. They further discovered that Mozi went through great difficulties, and would rather die than fail, so they used the glorious personal character of Mozi to serve as

以毕沅、孙诒让的研究成果影响最大。

毕沅是第一个综合他人成果而为《墨子》全书系统做注的人，他在自己撰写的《墨子注序》中充分肯定了墨学的价值，认为墨子的学说"通达经权，不可訾议"❶。而孙诒让更是耗费十年精力撰成这一时期墨学研究的巅峰之作——《墨子间诂》。清代古文大家俞樾称赞这部著作"自有墨子以来，未有此书"❷。

通过这些学者的研究和宣传，沉寂了两千年的墨学终于迎来了复兴的第一缕曙光。鸦片战争之后，随着西方文化的不断入侵下的民族危机的加深，当国内的一些学者们惊喜地发现《墨子》中有与西方科学类似的东西的时候，便迫不及待地举起了墨家的大旗以回击"西学东渐"的挑战。他们将墨学与西学完全等同，甚至想以此抵制西学的传播。其中，有邹伯奇首倡的"西学中源"说，认为西方的天文、历法、算学等都包含在《墨子》范围之内。而王闿运认为《墨子》是西方宗教之源，薛福成也认为西方耶稣之教起源于墨子。黄遵宪甚至还从五个方面考证了西学源自墨学，得出了"至于今日，而地球万国行墨之道者，十居其七"的结论。❸从科学、宗教到政治、伦理，当时的《墨子》几乎成为包罗万象的西学百科全书。种种牵强附会的议论，无不表现出这一时期墨学研究的缺陷和功利性。

甲午战争之后，无论是改良派还是革命派都深刻意识到，要想拯救风雨飘摇的中华民族，必须首先重铸伟大的国民精神。

❶ 参见孙中原：《墨学通论》，辽宁教育出版社，1993年，第326页。
❷ 参见孙中原：《墨学通论》，辽宁教育出版社，1993年，第327页。
❸ 参见程梅花，苏凤捷：《平民思想——〈墨子〉与中国文化》，河南大学出版社，2005年，第319页。

❶ See Sun Zhongyuan, *General Survey on Mohism*, Liaoning Education Press, 1993, p. 326.
❷ Ibid, p. 327.
❸ See Cheng Meihua and Su Fengjie, *The Thought of Commoners: Mozi and Chinese Culture*, Henan University Press, 2005, p. 319.

the example for the national character. On the foundation of the exegetical and commentarial work on *Mozi* by the Qian-Jia school, they continued to research and improve it, intending to include the superior ethics and morals of Mohism and Mozi's great spirit of sacrifice within their own system of ethics. This would arouse the citizenry to work in common to save the nation from subjugation.

In the reformist school, Liang Qichao can be termed the greatest disseminator of Mohism. He deeply felt Mozi's spirit that "made light of life and death" and that "endured pain and suffering." He raised a cry of warning, "If you want to save the China of today, how can you cast off the enduring of pain and suffering by Mohism? How can you cast off the making light of life and death of the Mohists?" [1] He not only highly praised the spirit of Mohism to save the world and rescue the people, he also for the first time placed Mohism within the system of western social science, adopting the research techniques of recent Western science to investigate Mohism. This provided a brand new look at things of the time.

After Liang Qichao, Hu Shi gained outstanding results in the field of Mohist studies. He for the first time used systematic logic to undertake research that gained splendid achievements in studying the *Mozi*, and especially in the field of the section called the "Mohist Canon." He claimed that the *Mozi* was the only work in the pre-Qin period "to have true value." [2] He also fully confirmed the value and position of the study of logic in the "Mohist Canon" section in the history of ancient Chinese philosophy and in the history of world logical studies, praising it for its contribution as the "most systematic and flourishing theory of the logical method in China." [3]

Under the impulse provided by Liang Qichao and Hu Shi, more and more scholars began to study and investigate Mozi, so the field of Mohist studies also produced the flourishing prospect of having many different trends of interpretation with a hundred flowers of different views blooming. A scholarly school that has been lost for thousands of years at last experienced a great restoration. And Mozi, the sage of a renowned school, with his great character of saving the world and succoring the people and his profound yet incisive learning, once again emitted his eye-catching colors on the great Chinese landscape.

他们又找到了赴汤蹈火、死不旋踵的墨子，以墨子的光辉人格作国民人格的榜样，并在乾嘉学派整理、注释《墨子》的基础上继续研究与改造它，希图把墨学中的优秀的伦理道德和墨子伟大的奉献精神揉入他们的理论之中，以唤醒国民共同救亡图存。

在改良派中，梁启超可谓是宣传墨学的最有力者。他深感于墨子"轻生死"、"忍痛苦"的救世精神，大声疾呼："欲救今日之中国，舍墨学之忍痛苦何以哉，舍墨学之轻生死何以哉！"❶他不仅高扬墨家精神以救世济民，而且第一次把墨学纳入西方社会科学体系之中，采用西方近代科学研究方法研究墨学，在当时给人以耳目一新之感。

继梁启超之后，胡适在墨学领域也取得了杰出的成就。他首次用系统的逻辑方法对《墨子》尤其是《墨经》进行了卓有成效的研究。他称《墨子》是先秦时期"真正有价值的唯一著作"❷，并充分肯定了《墨经》逻辑学在中国古代哲学史和世界逻辑学史上的地位和价值，称其为"为中国贡献了逻辑方法的最系统的发达学说"❸。

在梁启超、胡适的带动之下，越来越多的学者开始学墨、治墨，墨学研究领域也开始出现百家争鸣、百花齐放的繁荣景象。千年绝学终于迎来了伟大复兴，墨子——一代显学之圣，以他济世救民的伟大人格和博大精深的学术思想，在中华大地上再次绽放出夺目的光彩。

❶ 梁启超：《子墨子学说》，《饮冰室合集》第八卷专集之三十七，中华书局，1989年，第48页。
❷ 胡适：《先秦名学史》，学林出版社，1983年，第52页。
❸ 胡适：《先秦名学史》，学林出版社，1983年，第111页。

❶ Liang Qichao, "The intellectual theories of Master Mozi," in *Complete Works from the Studio for Drinking Iced Drinks*, Chapter 8, Special Collection 37, Zhonghua Book Co., 1989, p. 48.
❷ Hu Shi, *The History of Logic in the Pre-Qin Period*, Academia Press, 1983, p. 52.
❸ Ibid, p. 111.

受墨子思想影响很深的《礼记》书影，
《礼记》是中国古代知识分子的必读书
Picture of *The Book of Rites* Deeply Influenced by Mozi's Thought,
a Must Book for Intellectuals' Reading in Ancient China

十四 绵延千年，精神不灭

——墨学的影响

Chapter XIV A Thousand Years of Continuity, His Undying Spirit: The Influence of Mohism

Intellectual schools were numerous during the Spring and Autumn Period, and they all vied for attention. Although the questions that concerned each school and the issues they pursued were different within the larger social environment, inescapably there were points of correspondence among them. They assimilated and absorbed from each other. And in the course of mutual rebuttal and criticism, they were affected by the orientation of each other's intellectual thought and values. As a prominent school among the great states of the time, Mohism likewise exerted a broad and profound influence.

To a certain degree, Mencius absorbed Mozi's political thought that emphasized the people's welfare, and started to treat the economic issues of "regulating the people's production" and "lightening corvee labor and reducing taxes." He also took a clear stand against wars of annexation of the time, clearly advocating the position that "there were no righteous wars during the Spring and Autumn Period." ❶ He approved condemning rulers who committed crimes and opposed plundering the mass of innocent people, which was cut from the same cloth as Mozi's thought on opposing offensive warfare. Mencius said, "The people are the most precious, next comes the state, and the lord least of all." ❷ Whether a ruler was able to gain the support of the empire depended on whether he was able to first benefit the people and gain their support. This thought based on the people's welfare obviously was influenced by Mozi's views on the people's welfare.

The classic canonized by Confucians known as the *Book of Rites* was also deeply influenced by Mohism. The opening section of *The Book of Rites*, "Liyun" states, "When the great way was pursued, a public and common spirit ruled the world; they chose men of talent, virtue and ability. Their words were sincere and what they cultivated was harmony. Thus men did not love their parents only, nor treat as children only their own sons. A competent provision was secured for the aged till their death, employment for the able-bodied, and the means of growing up to the young." Comparing this to the thought in "Universal Love," Part Two of "For this reason, the old who lack wives or children will be supported until the end of their live; the young, weak and orphaned children will have the means to grow up," we can find the ideals demonstrated by both passages seem to be almost cut from the same cloth. Yet what the three sections of "Universal Love" adumbrates is precisely the utopian conception of Mencius' "do not only regard your own father as your father; do not only regard your own son as your son."

Legalists also absorbed much nutriment from the Mohists. Mozi advocated the idea of "Identifying with One's Superior," for the first time

春秋战国时期，学派林立，百家争鸣。在同一个社会大环境下，各个学派关注和探讨的问题虽各不相同，却也不乏相互契合之处。不同学派彼此间相互吸取、相互渗透，并在相互驳难，互相批判的过程中，受到对方学术思想和价值取向的影响。作为当时蜚声列国的显学之一，墨学对其他学派也有着广泛而深刻的影响。

孟子就在一定程度上吸取了墨子重民利的实利主义政治思想，开始关注"制民之产"和"轻徭薄赋"这样的经济问题。他还旗帜鲜明地反对当时的兼并战争，明确提出"春秋无义战"❶的说法，赞成诛伐有罪之君，反对掠夺无辜之民，这与墨子的非攻思想如出一辙。孟子说："民为贵，社稷次之，君为轻"❷，以能否为人民兴利、得到人民的拥护作为君王能否得到天下的根据。这样的民本思想显然是受到墨子的民本观念的影响。

被儒家奉为经典的《礼记》也深受墨学影响。春秋晚期青铜器夫差盂《礼记·礼运》开篇就说："大道之行也，天下为公，选贤与能，讲信修睦。故人不独亲其亲，不独子其子，使老有所终，壮有所用，幼有所长，矜寡孤独废疾者皆有所养。"将其与《兼爱下》中的"是以老而无妻子者，有所侍养以终其寿；幼弱孤童之无父母者，有所放依以长其身"相对比，二者所描述的理想境界几乎如出一辙。而《兼爱》三篇所阐发的，正是"不独亲其亲，不独子其子"的大同思想。

法家也从墨家那里吸收了许多思想养料。墨子倡导"尚同"说，第一次提出了政治上集权、思想上统一的原则，并称之为

---

❶《孟子·尽心下》。
❷《孟子·尽心下》。

❶ *Mencius*, "Jinxin," Part Two.
❷ *Mencius*, "Jinxin," Part Two.

proposing the principles of a centralized polity and unified thought. He described this as "the basis of enacting government and the essential element of rule." ❶ Yet what the Legalists advocated was "implementation is carried out among the four quarters, but the essential element is in the center. The sage grasps the essential, and the four directions carry it into effect." ❷ Upon close examination, this is the same result achieved by a different method in Mozi's theory of "Identifying with One's Superior." Additionally, Han Feizi further proposed the "monarch-centered theory" of "might is the chariot of the Lord; awe is the whip of the lord; ministers are the horses of the lord; the people are the wheels of the lord." ❸ It may be said that Han Feizi's theory of despotism was directly impacted by Mohist thinking on "Identifying with One's Superior."

Ever since Emperor Wu of Han "dismissed all other schools of philosophy and solely venerated Confucianism," Mohism was derided as a heresy. From a renowned school of thought, it became a lost school of thought. Although Mohism no longer existed as a scholarly school, Moist thought and spirit never fell into oblivion. Over the course of the next two thousand years, it continued to remain submerged within the tides of history, partly invisible and partly detectable in many intellectual realms within Chinese culture. It thus formed an important component of traditional Chinese culture.

After Liu Bang led the peasant revolutionary army into the Chinese heartland, he devised a few simple rules for all concerned in consultation with local elders: "Those who kill are executed, those who injure or rob others are punished appropriately." The obvious source for this was the "Mohist Code" promulgated internally as "Those who kill are executed, those who injure others are punished." ❹ The notion of Chen Sheng that "Should the noblemen be born talented people" is cut from the same cloth as Mohist's thought of "There is no permanent position of nobility among officials, there is no permanent low status for commoners." Many of the slogans and much of the thinking that emerged from among historical peasant uprisings are similar to Mohist slogans and thought. Therefore, Mohist thought formed a formidable intellectual weapon for peasant uprisings and peasant battles over the course of Chinese history.

An additional example is the wandering knight-errants as described by Sima Qian as "Their word is their bond, they always do what they say, their promises are always fulfilled. They do not cherish their own lives, but sacrifice themselves to save others." ❺ This spirit of chivalry obviously is indebted to what Mozi stressed as "Their word is their bond, they always do what they

"为政之本，治之要也" ❶。而法家"事在四方，要在中央。圣人执要，四方求效" ❷ 的主张，细细看来也与墨子的尚同论有着异曲同工之妙。此外，韩非子还提出了"势者君之车也，威者君之策也，臣者君之马也，民者君之轮也" ❸ 的"君主中心论"。可以说，韩非子的君主专制主义对墨家的"尚同"思想有着直接的继承关系。

自汉武帝"罢黜百家，独尊儒术"之后，墨学被斥为异端，由"显学"变成了"绝学"。虽然作为一个学派，墨家已不复存在，但墨家的思想和精神并没有被湮没。在此后的两千多年间，它仍沉潜在历史潮流之中，若隐若现于中华文化的多个思想领域，成为构成中国传统文化的重要内容。

刘邦率领农民起义军入关时，曾与关中父老约法三章："杀人者死，伤人及盗抵罪。"这显然来源于墨家内部奉行的"杀人者死，伤人者刑"的"墨者之法" ❹。陈胜的"王侯将相宁有种乎"与墨家的"官无常贵，而民无终贱"的思想几乎如出一辙。历代农民起义战争中都会出现与墨家相近的口号和思想，于是墨家思想就成了中国历史上农民起义和农民战争有力的思想武器。

还有司马迁笔下的游侠，"其言必信，其行必果，已诺必诚，不爱其躯，赴士之厄困。" ❺ 这种"任侠"精神显然受到墨子所强调的"言必信，行必果"的影响。此外，墨家思想中

---

❶《尚同下》。
❷《韩非子·扬权》。
❸《太平御览》卷620引《韩非子》佚文。
❹《吕氏春秋·去私》。
❺《史记·游侠列传》。

❶ "Identifying with One's Superior, Part Two."
❷ *Han Feizi*, "Yangquan."
❸ *Taiping Imperial Encyclopaedia*, Chapter 620, citing a loss passage from *Han Feizi*.
❹ *The Spring and Autumn Annals of Mr. Lü*, "Qusi."
❺ *The Records of the Grand Historian*, "The Biographies of the Wandering Knights."

say." Additionally, the concepts of "embracing mutual love," "suffering for the sake of righteousness," being willing to go through fire and floods for the sake of all the people of the world, as well as "bringing about benefit to the world and eliminating evil in the world" within Mohist thought all deeply impacted chivalrous knight-errants throughout Chinese history. Such chivalrous spirit within organizations among the Chinese people such as "save the world and eradicate violence" and "within the four seas all men are brothers" as well as the spirit of mutual aid as helping each other out of difficulties and drawing one's sword in the cause of justice, are all manifestations of Mohist character to a large degree.

Mohist sentiments of being against fatalism and struggling on one's own, opposing empty theorizing and stressing practical action, and the nature of Chinese to struggle and strive for in a pragmatic manner are all intimately tied in with this Mohist character. Mozi's advocacy of hard work and frugality to an even greater degree, deeply percolated throughout the psychology of the Chinese people, forming one of the admirable virtues of the Chinese race. Mozi was against offensive warfare, and the Chinese race has always loved peace and opposed aggression against others. At the same time, Mohist military theory of active defense has likewise molded the Chinese race's spiritual nature of unyielding defiance of violence and bravery in opposing all foreign aggression. Besides the Mohist's early advocacy of the scientific spirit became a strong force promoting the development of ancient science and technology.

Although over the centuries Mohists have been criticized as a heretical school that few cared to study, nevertheless from Confucianism down to the knight-errants among the people, all segments of society have either consciously or unconsciously absorbed and transmitted the theories and spirit of Mohism. It may be said that the Mohism which became "lost" was never ever truly lost; it remained latent within the Chinese race as an imperceptible influence, silently flowing within the blood of the Chinese people.

的"兼相爱","自苦以为义"、为了天下万民的利益而赴汤蹈火、以及"兴天下之利，除天下之害"等内容也都深深感染了中国历代的侠义之士。中国民间社党"济世除暴"、"四海之内皆兄弟"等侠义精神，以及中国人路见不平、拔刀相助的助人精神，在很大程度上也都是墨家人格精神的体现。

墨家非命而尚力，反对空谈而强调实行，而中国人勤奋务实的品质也与此有着密切关系。墨子倡导的勤劳节俭，更是深深积淀于中国人的民族心理之中，成为整个民族的优良品德之一。墨子非攻，而中华民族也一向爱好和平、反对侵略。与此同时，墨家积极防御的军事理论同样陶冶了中华民族不畏强暴、勇于反抗一切外来侵略的不屈不挠的精神品质。而由墨家首倡的科学精神，也已经成为推动中国古代科技发展的强大动力。

虽然千百年来墨学一直被斥为异端而少人问津，但是，从正统的儒学到民间的侠士，都在自觉不自觉地吸取和传承着墨家学说和墨家精神。可以说，"中绝"的墨家从来就没有消失过，它以一种隐性潜在的方式暗暗影响着中华民族，默默流淌在每一个中国人的血液之中。

Translator's Note

This biography of Mozi is the third translation I have done for the *Collection of Critical Biographies of Chinese Thinkers*, Concise Edition, Chinese-English. In some respects it is the most satisfying. Professor Zheng Jiewen and Zhang Qian reduced Xing Zhaoliang's original text in a most admirable manner, with the intricacies of Mozi's thought explained clearly and concisely. This is to be expected given the high quality of all the volumes in this set as insured by the editors-in-chief Zhou Xian and Cheng Aimin. What made this translation especially appealing to me personally was first, the intrinsic interest of the subject. Mozi offered a very viable alternative to the Confucian vision of the Way, an alternative that appealed to the common man. Aptitude, effort, and a working-man's skills were the keys to success in travelling this path, a different set of skills than the moral rectitude, ritual mastery and intimate connections that success in the Confucian realm demanded. The relevancy of Mohist thought to the modernization of China and its contributions to world science add great interest to the story of Mohism. All in all, students of Chinese thought will find Mozi a unique voice among the Hundred Schools that demands to be heard even today.

Another reason that this translation was so satisfying to me personally was because no other reduction in the set has so skillfully set the abstract world of thought so solidly within the concrete customs and culture of a particular region, in this case the Zhulou Culture of Shandong. Despite the technical nature of chapter one and a resultant dryness for a few page, the theoretical reasoning behind Mozi's practical policies were tied together with a sureness that informed both thought and act. Such a close look at ancient material culture and the thinking it produced is a unique multidimensional view of the past rarely afforded a modern student of Chinese history and philosophy. It is also a model that should be followed more often.

Mozi has been neglected too long by students of Chinese philosophy. With the publication of this bilingual biography, students will find an accessible yet informative entrance into the life and teachings of this most modern of all ancient philosophers.

Dr. David B. Honey
Brigham Young University
Monkey Day (December 14, 2010)

图书在版编目(CIP)数据

墨子:汉英对照/郑杰文,张倩著;(美)霍尼
(Honey, D.)译. —南京:南京大学出版社,2010.12
(中国思想家评传简明读本:中英文版)
ISBN 978-7-305-07970-2

Ⅰ.①墨… Ⅱ.①郑…②张…③霍… Ⅲ.①墨翟(
前480~前420)—评传—汉、英 Ⅳ.①B224

中国版本图书馆CIP数据核字(2010)第256937号

出版发行　南京大学出版社
社　　址　南京汉口路22号　邮　编　210093
网　　址　http://www.NjupCo.com
出版人　左　健

丛　书　名　《中国思想家评传》简明读本(中英文版)
书　　名　墨　子
著　　者　郑杰文　张　倩
译　　者　David B. Honey
审　　读　李　寄
责任编辑　芮逸敏　　　　编辑热线　025-83593947

照　　排　江苏凤凰制版印务中心
印　　刷　江苏凤凰通达印刷有限公司
开　　本　787×1092　1/16　印张13　字数198千
版　　次　2010年12月第1版　2010年12月第1次印刷
ISBN 978-7-305-07970-2
定　　价　28.00元

发行热线　025-83594756　83686452
电子邮箱　Press@NjupCo.com
　　　　　Sales@NjupCo.com (市场部)